PICKING UP THE OPTIONS

# picking
# up the
# options

HAROLD HOWE II

Department of Elementary School Principals • National Education Association

NEA stock number: Paper, 181-05574; Cloth, 181-05576

Library of Congress catalog card number: 68-58909

Single copies, paper, $6.00; cloth, $7.50
2-9 copies, 10% discount; 10 or more copies, 20% discount

Published by the DEPARTMENT OF ELEMENTARY SCHOOL PRINCIPALS,
National Education Association, Washington, D. C. 20036

Printed in the United States of America

Design and Composition by THE WILLIAM BYRD PRESS, INC.
Printing by STEPHENSON LITHOGRAPH, INC.

# TABLE
# OF
# CONTENTS

# FOREWORD

Men in positions of national leadership are called upon so frequently to address major gatherings that they find it impossible to meet these demands with speeches that deal freshly with important issues. Harold Howe II, United States Commissioner of Education, is an outstanding exception. The 23 addresses presented here were delivered within a span of two years. They contain recurrent theses, but each speech is unique in its emphasis and development. Individually and collectively, they furnish new insights on critical issues and invoke increased concern and effort to approach more nearly our great aspirations for American education.

This nation—and much of the world—is experiencing profound social changes. Education is repeatedly identified as the primary means for preparing individuals to participate in the changing society and for helping society itself to develop and maintain dynamic stability. As the key importance of education for all persons is recognized, new educational goals are articulated, new problems in achieving these goals are identified, and new power centers emerge—power centers seeking to influence the development and control of schools and colleges. In this period of flux, steadfastness of purpose and clarity of vision are frequently lacking. Howe's straightforward comments cut through the confusion, and his firm but kindly admonitions renew our sense of purpose.

In discussions of school desegregation, the education of disadvantaged children, and the plight of the ghettoes, Howe emphasizes justice and the welfare of the nation; he does not allow his audience the opportunity to dismiss his ideas as sentimental, or as idealistic beyond reason. On such a variety of subjects as early childhood education, individualized instruction, work experience for adolescents, the education of teachers, the limitations of scholastic aptitude tests, educational technology, and the values of humanistic education, Howe expresses continuing concern for the fullest development of the individual and the opening of doors for all children. He is sharply critical of unimaginative and insensitive school programs that set frustrating limits on the aspirations and achievements of human beings.

At a time when many fear that we are departing from the established doctrine of local control of education and are alarmed over the possibility of federal intervention in school matters, he reminds us of the opportunity which local, state, and federal partnerships offer to develop more adequate, more effective, and more meaningful education—not by having any one of the partners relinquish its role but by each assuming greater responsibility and making greater efforts to deal with the problems we face. The school he envisions is a school no longer isolated from the larger community but open in ways that enable children to move easily from learning in school to learning in the community, with people from many parts of society serving the broad aims of the school and the diverse needs of the individual.

For every child, quality education is as necessary as adequate nutrition. Howe's basic theme is the necessity—*now*—to provide true equality of educational opportunity for all children. This is a major criterion for considering individual and state responsibility for education, for examining the opportunities to be seized by student activists, and for reassessing the role of the federal government in assuring the protection of the individual against unjust practices of the community.

Commissioner Howe's words are both wise and refreshing. His speeches reflect a strong sense of urgency and a persistent concern for the big problems that demand thoughtful and serious attention. At the same time, they are enlivened by a dry humor that adds to the enjoyment of reading them. The Office of Education deserves our appreciation for making these addresses available; the Department of Elementary School Principals, NEA, is to be congratulated for publishing them.

RALPH W. TYLER

# PICKING UP THE OPTIONS

# CHAPTER I

# PICKING UP THE OPTIONS

IN EXERCISING these options for change, the principal is often not the master of his own fate. He works in something called "the system," and much of what he does must accommodate itself to the headquarters operation. But there is a lot more room for differences among schools than most people are willing to admit.

From an address presented at the 1968 Annual Meeting of the Department of Elementary School Principals, NEA, Houston, Texas.

# PICKING UP THE OPTIONS

OF THE MANY HATS THE COMMISSIONER OF EDUcation must wear, the one I have chosen for this occasion is that of an agitator. Now an agitator is one who takes people who are contented with their lot and makes them dissatisfied. In the narrow sense, I suppose the word is almost always used as a term of reproach. It should not be. An agitator is also a person with a sense of mission—who insists that things as they stand are not good enough.

If we are to take any of the education legislation passed by Congress during the last four years seriously, all of us must get a little bit of the agitator in our blood. That is what the legislation calls for. It insists that school people push out wider borders, grow and move and explore new domains.

No act of Congress can by its wording bring about this kind of movement and change. What the legislation can and does do is give education an opportunity to stretch and change itself by creating new options for people at all levels and in all specialities—the teacher, the principal, the superintendent, the school board, the university president. It is the new options open to the elementary school that I want to discuss, because it is in the elementary school that all effective movement must start.

The first subject on which I want to agitate is preschool education. As we learn more about the learning process, all indicators point to early childhood education as the option we most need to pick up. Laboratory schools, private and cooperative nurseries, day-care centers, early education for the handicapped—all have contributed a rich body of information on the behavior of four- and five-year-olds. We have welcomed research from these sources into the literature for almost 50 years, but only about three-fifths of America's children below age six have the chance for kindergarten, and the number attending school below age five remains negligible.

Few of our present arrangements for bringing younger children into a school-type setting are designed primarily as a systematic approach to beginning learning and to developing the skills and sensitivities on which learning depends. College and university laboratory schools are first of all research and teacher training enterprises. Day-care centers and many nursery schools are set up primarily to care for children of working mothers. For the most part, it has only been the relatively well-to-do who—over the years—have been able to afford early childhood education planned for the sake of the intellectual opportunities it offers. Only recently have we begun to recognize that early education is a necessary enrichment for youngsters from much different, less favored circumstances—youngsters with restricted language skills, with few models in the home likely to lead toward success with the requirements of school. For them, early education is the first step toward any hope for success. But increasing evidence shows that it must be early education with a plan and a purpose beyond socialization and custodial care.

A survey of some day-care arrangements for young Negro children in North Carolina showed a pattern in which mothers placed their infants for $1 a day with another mother whose job was running a day-care center, a job she was likely to take because of lack of competence to do anything else. Taking in from five to fifteen children of other working mothers, this locally developed day-care center started the process of educational deprivation. It rewarded those children who remained passive, who didn't move about and exhibit curiosity, who didn't ask questions. By the time a child has been in such an institution for two or three years, his sensibilities have been diminished, not stimulated. He has learned, through a vicious system of rewards for limiting the development of his faculties, a kind of behavior which will guarantee his failure in school.

New amendments to the Social Security Act will give states and communities an opportunity to alter the character of some of these day-care centers. The legislation makes substantial matching funds available to support day-care facilities for dependent children whose mothers are working or are in job training programs. These, of course, are the children who most need the kind of meaningful instruction I've been talking about and I think this new money will get us started at giving it to them. I see no reason why states or communities can't combine some of this new welfare money with money from the Elementary and Secondary Education Act to turn the day-care centers into early education centers. When administrative details are worked out, you will be hearing more about federally sponsored day-care centers. It is quite possible many of them will be adjuncts of the elementary school and that you will have a hand in planning the programs.

We do not know exactly how to guarantee success in education for the severely deprived youngster, but we do know something of the attitudes and feelings and experiences that get fixed in a child before the school years and determine his disposition toward and readiness for formal learning. It seems clear that if we are to make any appreciable headway, we will have to reach him well before the present school entrance age. Powerful evidence indicates that the level of intellectual achievement is half determined by age four and another 30 percent is predictable at age seven.

John Fischer of Teachers College, Columbia University, puts it this way: "There is no ground for believing that a child's academic fate is sealed by his seventh birthday, but it means that any community that seriously wants to improve its children's opportunities will start them to school early. In terms of sheer economy, it can be shown that the earlier the investment in systematic intellectual development is begun, the greater will be the rate of return."

I know of several preschool programs that have been superbly successful with deprived children. And this, I think, has much to do with the education of children in general. From our concern with the extremely disadvantaged child, from our search for ways to educate him, may come a change in the quality of education of all children.

Hopefully, we will find a satisfactory way for the elementary school to relate to the broad movement we call preschool education. In fact, we might do well to phase out the term "preschool" education and start asking ourselves how our present elementary structure can expand and change itself to embrace school children who might be five or four or three years old.

I would predict that by the year 2000 most children in the United States will be attending regular public school starting at age four. If things run true to form, the "experts" will still be arguing about whether it is a good idea to start formal learning that early, but the new frontiers of the elementary school will then be among the three-year-olds, many of whom will be going to school at home on TV.

We are not completely without models for these future developments. Head Start, operated by the Office of Economic Opportunity, is the most publicized. Stimulated by the experiences of Head Start, many school systems have been moved to pattern their own programs after it with Office of Education funds available under Title I of the Elementary and Secondary Education Act. We have had three years with this type of early education experience—with most programs marked by a permissive quality and more emphasis on changing environment and attitudes than on the teaching of specific skills. The assumption has been that children with deprived home backgrounds can catch up *indirectly*.

Now we are testing some unconventional approaches—the most significant being based on the proposition that deprivation means mainly language deprivation and that we had better set about approaching that problem *directly* at an early age with a variety of techniques, including intensive drill.

The controversial Bereiter-Engelmann experiment, conducted

at the University of Illinois with a grant from the Office of Education, is a case in point. The design is to give deprived children what they need most—the ability to express themselves and to work with numbers—and give it to them in a highly structured, no-nonsense setting. The technique has been described as akin to programed learning—without the hardware. It is a rigid and efficient speed-up system. It has also raised IQ's and achievement scores phenomenally. Those who support the theory behind this type of project admit that the children are under stress, but they say it is the stress of succeeding at something hard rather than the debilitating stress of failure. They report that along with achievement comes a gain in the kind of self-respect and motivation required to compete during the rest of the school years. I am not beating a drum for this particular technique. I am merely acknowledging that it has raised some questions as well as some eyebrows, and saying that we cannot ignore its findings. From experiments such as this, and there have been a few by now, we are gathering evidence to help us decide what kind of preschool experience is most successful with children who have excessive catching up to do—the kind that stresses cognitive learning or the kind that operates in the tradition of the nursery school.

If I read the signals accurately, this whole area of early education will be a major emphasis for the next several decades. And it will call for a tremendous adjustment not only in the school structure but in the administration and the philosophy of the principal.

The second point to which I would draw your attention is the role of the school as a training ground for teachers. NEA President Braulio Alonso recently defined the new principal as a curriculum innovator, expediter, morale builder, facilitator, delegator, and organizer. I would add to that the duty of director of a teacher training institution, for each elementary school has built into it the potential for developing and changing teaching skills.

Traditionally, the elementary school is thought of as a place where future teachers can come from the universities to do their practice teaching. But it has a much broader role as a staff-development institution. In fact, I would say it must become a "self-renewing" enterprise, training and retraining a variety of educational personnel for its own staff and for service in the many other elements of education, including the operation of government-sponsored programs.

Particularly in the training of teachers and teacher aides who will work with four- and five-year-olds, the elementary school has a chance for a new mission. No institution has yet carved out the training of these teachers as its private preserve, so that the chance still remains to train them in the way that makes the most sense—right in the school itself.

Now when I speak of staff development, I am not talking about two or three meetings a month held at four o'clock in the afternoon for a group of people who are physically and mentally exhausted from contending with 35 children for six hours. That is an exercise in futility. What is needed is a new set of arrangements that will bring people who serve children together during the course of the school day—a situation where teachers as well as children are learning from one another.

It seems to me that the school itself has many of the necessary components for taking on the teacher training responsibility. For one thing, it offers a more practical setting than the college—the presence of a pupil population, a principal, direct contact with parents, and a community environment. All these are factors that take training out of the abstract and make it visible and concrete.

I am not preaching the demise of teacher training institutions. They are working at change, too, and the newest piece of federal education legislation—the Education Professions Development Act—offers them some elbowroom and wherewithal to explore and create and change their course. But I am saying that there exists in every school an untapped training resource—and that resource is represented by your best teachers. I think we have learned enough through our experiences with team teaching to know that when we bring teachers into working association, they learn from one another. New teachers, and teachers who are not as effective as others, can, by working in combination with your most effective teachers, gain expertise or refurbish their skills.

Staff-development programs can be arranged in cooperation with universities, but this is not always necessary. They need not be confined within the walls of a single building either. All kinds of devices can be used to take advantage of strengths the schools already possess in their very best teachers. Intensive visitation programs can be arranged so that the best teachers from a number of schools can demonstrate their talents and techniques and approaches. Teacher aides who may eventually become teachers might start their preparation in this way through observation. An effective teacher can demonstrate everything from teaching reading to the best use of nonprofessionals. And this may be the only way to transmit those subtle elements of attitude and sensitivity and confidence needed by every successful teacher. In the light of what we know about the significance of good teaching in the earliest years, perhaps we ought to go at this type of enterprise most systematically with our teachers of four-, five-, and six-year-olds.

How do you go about the sticky business of selecting the most effective teachers and tapping them for a position of status? Every principal knows who his best teachers are. If I asked you to name them right now, I don't think you would have to hesitate a moment. But principals have tended to shy away from establishing a hierarchy or creating distinctions among their staff— probably because that sort of thing has generally been associated with merit pay proposals, of which teachers are suspicious. Yet we *are* moving toward a hierarchy among the teachers, at least in some schools. That is what team teaching is all about. That is what is implicit in the Teacher Corps. That is the arrangement in the project which has been launched in 40 school districts as part of the new Follow Through program sponsored by Office of Education funds. Unless human ingenuity has gone completely bankrupt, it seems to me that ways can be found to identify your best teachers and use their skills in training others without creating invidious distinctions. Doctors do it; lawyers do it; other professions do it; why can't teachers?

In every inner-city school system we find a cadre of excellent teachers—many of them prepared just as much by temperament and professional commitment as by anything they learned at college. These are the people who expect and enable children to succeed when others would give up—who can communicate with white and Negro ghetto children and win response. And they are not necessarily people who have emerged from the ghetto themselves. They *are* individuals who feel at home in their classrooms and can create an atmosphere for learning, sometimes in spite of a "system" that confines and inhibits them. I have heard some of these teachers say that to do the job, they feel compelled to close the doors of their classrooms, to lock out the rest of the school. Yet these are the teachers we most need to bring out of their isolation so that they can create others in their mold.

If the elementary schools take up this option of getting into the teacher training business, they will not have to be concerned about the "brain drain" to other education enterprises. They will be recreating good teachers all the time, and a good school needs to do just that.

The third subject on which I want to agitate is the principal's relationship to the federally supported education programs. American education is on the brink of its second great feat. The first had to do with opening the schools to all children. The second has to do with truly *educating* them all.

As principals try to adapt their schools to treat children in the variety of ways their differences require, they will find themselves increasingly involved with Federal programs. This is not to suggest that you hurry to install a hot line to Washington. It does mean that you will be on both the giving and receiving ends of programs developed by your local agency, your state, or a nearby university with support from the Office of Education.

Ideally, you will cooperate with your teachers and your superintendent in the development of proposals that will receive support from federal funds. I say "ideally," for I do not think that principals—or teachers for that matter—have had sufficient opportunity to share in the initial development of programs supported by the federal government. As federal programs bring the schools and the colleges of teacher education into closer alliance, you may have the chance to plow back into the training curriculum something of your experience or to participate in some other cooperative arrangement. I hope that you will insist on such participation.

I doubt that it is necessary to understand fully all of the back and forth motion among local, state, and federal agencies in administering the programs. It is important, however, to understand the intent of all this activity—to understand that federal education programs are aimed at buttressing particular aspects of the education enterprise of significance throughout the nation, to understand that they are intended to help schools reach for the level of quality which our national interests and ideals require.

This is not a matter of the Congress or the Administration saying to state or local officials, "We know better than you do what your schools need." Rather, it is a device for the development of school programs which address themselves to national problems likely to be overlooked unless federal funds are provided for them. With very few exceptions, school activities financed by the Office of Education involve local initiative at the outset and state approval as a second step. I must say that the best proposals are those that reflect the ideas and experiences of the principals and teachers in the schools. And I suspect that it is these programs that work out best in the classroom.

The federal government is making and will continue to make a substantial contribution to increasing the investment per child in those schools where special services are necessary to overcome the effects of a deprived home environment and to backing experiments in more effective education for all children. This money is being used in a variety of creative ways to individualize instruction, to broaden the child's experiences, to increase verbal and other skills. In using these funds, you are frequently dealing with youngsters who have nothing in their previous experience that would encourage them to value these skills highly. As I said earlier, we really do not know how to make all children receptive to learning. Even if we have a fair measure of success at raising a youngster's test score, we are not always doing the far more important job of improving his behavior, arming him with skills and information he can connect with something in the real world, and making him eager to develop those skills further. I think we have to give considerable thought to how we can work this energizing element into the school program.

One way, of course, is to make the school a part of the community—to bring some of what is familiar into the school and put something of the school's values into the home and community where a major share of learning takes place. The suburban elementary school typically enjoys an open relationship with the community. It has capitalized on the intensive interest many of its parents display during the first years of their children's schooling. Yet in the poverty neighborhoods the public school too often stands in isolation, physically and emotionally. Ghetto parents may mistrust it and fear it. To some parents it seems to diminish their children, and to diminish them—the parents—by making their children unsuccessful. In some places the alienation is so strong that parents are advocating the elimination of public schools and the development of other kinds of schools. Such feelings are perhaps an inevitable outcome of the big city crisis—of the uncertainty and anxiety of ghetto residents.

In all communities—rural and suburban, but especially inner-city—the principal needs to take the initiative in tailoring his school to the character of the community. He needs to solicit parent participation and to help parents understand what kinds of contributions they can make. The principal ought to be welcoming parents and letting them see how the school is run and explaining to them its policies and programs. He should at the same time be converting the school into a community resource that offers adults a center for community activities, instruction in practical subjects as well as leisure-time activities. The school should become the center for operating community projects, for discussing such down-to-earth matters as housing standards and the enforcement of health regulations.

When I say the principal "ought to" I mean he ought to use his authority to get these things done. And that in turn means having qualified personnel to whom such responsibilities can be delegated. It also means persuading his superintendent to make use of federal funds to accomplish these purposes.

Philadelphia has the right idea, I think. The city is using some of its Title I money to hire community residents—all active in church or civic groups and all fairly well known in the neighborhoods—to help parents with problems, to bring them into activities conducted at the school, to integrate social services, and in general to act as a link between the educational system and the people it is trying to serve. These "school-community coordinators," as Philadelphia calls them, report to the principal and work under his direction.

Different patterns are needed in different communities, but if the ghetto school is to perform its educational function, I don't think there is any viable alternative to creating an alliance with the community.

In exercising these options for change, the principal is often not the master of his own fate. He works in something called "the system," and much of what he does must accommodate itself to the headquarters operation. But there is a lot more room for differences among schools than most people are willing to admit. A good school system does not impose a lock-step order on its schools. Principals should have authority and they should exercise it, as instructional leaders and as administrators.

One of the high quality school systems I know—that of Newton, Massachusetts, where I was once a principal—has a sensible philosophy for getting quality in its schools. The idea is simply to hire good people and turn them loose—restricted only by the obligation to remain in communication with the rest of the school system and the knowledge that what they do will be evaluated honestly. By and large, I back that philosophy.

I began by saying I planned to make you dissatisfied—perhaps I should have said dissatisfied with the lot of the schools. I hope I have done that, and I hope I have also pointed up some of the options that are open as you move and explore and reach for new successes. I cannot predict an uncomplicated future for the elementary principal, but I can envision a dramatic and significant one.

# CHAPTER 2

# RECRUITING FOR THE NEW PARTNERSHIP

W E ALL pay the price for our national failures, whether those failures be reflected in a slow start in the
space race or in a high rate of unemployment. So it makes good sense for us
to pool our resources throughout our
society and at every level of government
to insure that no human talent is wasted.

From an address before the Georgia Vocational Association, Atlanta, Georgia, March 18, 1966.

# RECRUITING FOR
# THE NEW PARTNERSHIP

JUST AS MASSACHUSETTS GAVE BIRTH TO OUR FREE public schools, so Georgia has been the cradle of vocational education. The pioneering of Senator Hoke Smith and Representative Dudley Hughes in sponsoring the first Vocational Education Act half a century ago gave this kind of education a national impetus which has served us well ever since.

How is it serving us today? What is the state of vocational education in America in the mid-1960's? What are its prospects for the future? What tasks, finally, does the advancement of vocational education impose on us today?

Before addressing myself to these questions, I would like to issue a sort of amateur's manifesto. Being appointed Commissioner of Education imposes on such fortunate fellows as myself the necessity of commenting on a bewildering variety of educational matters. Not only does the Commissioner serve as the administration spokesman on education, he also receives questions from school children in Vermont about the desirability of studying Latin, from high schoolers in California about the propriety of Beatle haircuts, and from faculty members in Texas about the validity of foreign language requirements for the Ph.D. degree.

It is obvious that no one man can be a real authority on all these matters, so every Commissioner must forge his own compromise with these expectations of omniscience. At one extreme, he can confess his ignorance and smile helplessly; at the other, he can parrot the words of a specialist and hope that his ghost-written wisdom will inspire neither yawns nor a riot; or, finally, he can simply do his best to talk like a reasonably well-informed and educated man about a subject in which he has genuine interest.

It is this latter course that I choose this morning, and for the theme of my remarks I need go no further than to consider the composition of my audience, for you include not only educators from local school districts but also state and federal officials, businessmen, and other citizens interested in vocational education. This is a heterogeneous group, and its very variety reflects some of the most significant changes taking place in education today.

First, I would say that it suggests the growing strength of the local-state-federal partnership in education. The Constitution leaves education entirely in the hands of the states, and most states delegate a generous portion of this responsibility to local school districts. But our founding fathers did not assign any responsibility for education to the federal government.

In general, this exclusion of the central government has worked out well for American education. Despite the deficiencies in our schools—and certainly no one who reads the papers can be unaware of them—I believe it remains true that our free public school system has served the nation well. We can compare our system with the centralized arrangements in several European countries and conclude that local control is the best way to run the educational enterprise.

Nevertheless, as with any human arrangement, our educational setup has some weaknesses. For example, it makes it difficult for our schools to cope with population mobility.

According to the latest United States census, one American in five moves every year—out of his community, out of his county, out of his state. While testifying to the continuing sense of adventure in the American heart, this readiness to pull up stakes and chase the rainbow creates problems for our schools, for more important than the fact of the population shift itself is the character of that shift. We see it especially in our cities. The tendency there is for the upward-mobile, middle-class white, or middle-class Negro to leave the city for a home in the suburbs. At the same time, many poor and uneducated rural whites and Negroes are migrating to our cities.

As every educator knows, school finance is tied to taxes. The changing character of the city population has resulted in an erosion of the city tax base. While placing heavier demands on the city schools, in terms of an increasing population with an increasingly varied cultural background, the new migrants have brought less wherewithal in terms of earning power to help the city schools serve them properly.

This problem is not restricted to the cities. Rural areas have felt the same pinch, and they have in addition another problem: their population is scattered over a greater land area, so they have an even more difficult time concentrating the tax funds necessary to maintain good schools. What is more, these rural areas, which depend largely on agriculture, have experienced a mammoth displacement of their people through the scientific and technological revolution in farming.

Thus there is a kind of geographic imbalance in our local educational system. We can see its consequences in the paradox of outstanding schools on the fringe of a city and poor ones at the core. We can see it also in the different expenditures among the states for education. It is a fact of American life that there are rich states and poor ones, and we can trace these disparities in the quality of their schools.

It was this situation that brought the federal government into education in a big way, starting with the National Defense Education Act of 1958. It was this situation that led to the Vocational Education Act of 1963 and to the 23 other pieces of educational legislation that Congress has passed in the last three years alone.

These laws do not represent a new division of responsibility. The states and local agencies still retain control of education, and both Congress and President Johnson have stated their determination to preserve this traditional arrangement.

But these laws do reflect a new partnership in education among the local, state, and federal governments. They reflect, in addition, an awareness that this nation has a common life and that educational weaknesses in North Dakota or New Mexico affect Georgia and Illinois. We all pay the price for our national failures, whether those failures be reflected in a slow start in the space race or in a high rate of unemployment. So it makes good sense for us to pool our resources throughout our society and at every level of government to insure that no human talent is wasted.

The effects of this new partnership can already be seen in improved vocational education opportunities. Since 1963, the federal government has allocated more than $80 million for area vocational schools. Coupled with state and local contributions, this investment has led to the planning and construction of 208 area vocational schools in 41 States. Here in Georgia, you have completed 16 such schools and are building 9 more.

These new schools are as different from the conventional trade school of a decade ago as the latter was from the little red schoolhouse. They contain expensive machinery ranging from delicate computers to heavy earth-moving machines. They utilize such modern teaching devices as motion picture equipment and closed-circuit television. Unlike the dim educational warehouses of a generation ago, these new schools reflect aesthetic considerations in their construction, out of the conviction that a pleasant, attractive atmosphere aids learning.

But this partnership can do only half the job in vocational education. To complete the task that an increased governmental investment in education has begun, we must turn to a new partnership: that of the schools and industry. For the schools cannot of themselves and by themselves keep pace with the rapid changes in industry which determine the relevance of the vocational education curriculum. It is not so much the fact of change in industry which startles our national imagination today as the rate of that change.

For example, I suspect that many of us—particularly the humanities majors—regarded computers 10 years ago as electronic gimmicks. We felt that they made fascinating backdrops for science fiction programs on TV but were in reality little more than fancy adding machines.

And yet a report issued fully two years ago stated that computers can "diagnose symptoms for the physician, research a case for the lawyer, read envelopes for the postman, analyze market portfolios for the broker, and keep inventory for the merchant." Every one of those new functions puts a human being out of work. I understand that 50 statisticians in the Census Bureau do the same amount of work that required 4,000 people in 1950, that the check-writing staff in the Treasury Department has been reduced from 400 people to 4.

This is a staggering rate of change, and it places a staggering burden on our entire educational system, from prekindergarten to postgraduate. It is clear that if we are to train today's student for a useful life tomorrow, we must have some indication of what tomorrow will be like. Vocational schools must have much better information, not only on job opportunities today but also on job requirements 5, 10, and 20 years from now.

This, again, is one of the concerns of the federal government. After decades of trial and error in shaping education, we are placing a new emphasis on research. Vocational research coordinating units have been established in 24 states to assist state and local school agencies, colleges, universities, and non-profit organizations in conducting investigations of occupational training. The major concern of these units will be to study data on employment opportunities and trends in order to plan curricula, facilities, teacher training, recruitment, and placement. These units will also serve as clearinghouses of information for other state and local agencies to enable them to keep a closer check on the pulse of employment.

This is a major step in the right direction, but it emphasizes governmental action. We need to bring industry also into our planning. If our vocational schools are to fulfill the essential role a technological America expects of them, they must reflect the realities of industrial life. The most important single reality is change. Industry has learned to cope with change as a matter of sheer survival, and it has valuable lessons to pass on to our schools.

Those of you who have spent the bulk of your lives in vocational education know how narrowly many persons outside the field conceive your function. They think of vocational education as a process by which you confer manual dexterity, plain and simple.

I suspect that this criticism held true in the past, but it is very nearly obsolete now. The difference between vocational *education* and vocational *training* is not one of semantics but of course content and point of view. The student or worker is not simply a pair of hands; he is a person, with a claim to individual dignity, regardless of whether he makes a living over a lathe or in a library. The more sophisticated vocational education programs reflect this. They recognize that a man's education must prepare him for every aspect of life, not just for the time he spends on the job. These programs help the vocational student understand the relationship between his work and the total world in which he lives. I urge you to consider how the vocational education curriculum can be broadened to develop every student not simply as employee but as citizen, as father or mother, and as a distinctive human person with a life to live, as well as a living to earn. I suspect that to accomplish this, you will have to inject a balanced helping of the humanities into the vocational curriculum.

We are getting away from the notion that education is a neatly packaged period of years inserted into a person's life somewhere between his first pair of long pants and his first vote. Education no longer ends with a high school diploma or a college degree. I think within 25 years we will come to regard it as entirely natural for a person to return periodically to a college or a technical institution to renew and refresh his education.

That is why, for example, the marriage of adult and vocational education within one bureau of the U.S. Office of Education seems to me an eminently logical union. When we think of vocational education, there is no reason at all why we should think only of the teenager. In fact, we must not. We must think also of the older, semi-skilled worker who is anxious to elevate his abilities to a new plane of skill and understanding that makes him eligible for more demanding and more fulfilling work. We can depreciate a machine over a period of years and then junk it without serious loss. But we cannot depreciate humans, and we certainly must not junk them.

Industry can help our vocational schools to fashion training courses that confer a mental flexibility as well as manual dexterity. Collaboration between the businessman and the educator can teach us how to train a student, not simply for one job that might be automated out of existence in five years but for a career built on an understanding of the principles underlying a service or production process. Industry and education can investigate together the problem of retraining, of salvaging for a useful, fulfilling, and productive life those older workers whose skills have been made obsolete.

Far from removing any burden of educational leadership from individuals and local communities, the federal commitment to education offers even greater possibilities for initiative to every teacher, every school administrator, every businessman and citizen.

President Johnson said it in one sentence: "The federal government can provide leadership, information, and other assistance, but fundamentally it is action carried forward in each community that will decide how well we achieve our national objectives."

I hope each of you will consider how you can act to help achieve our national objectives. I hope each of you will devise new modes of cooperation between education and industry to strengthen a partnership that is as promising as it is young. For not only will that partnership benefit our schools, their graduates, and the businesses that depend on fresh infusions of youth, it will benefit also a nation composed of 50 states that share a common health—or a common frailty.

Today, even more than in 1917, the words of the old recruiting poster hold true: "Uncle Sam needs *you*." And he needs you not only in Washington but right here and right now.

# CHAPTER 3

# WHO'S IN CHARGE HERE?

THE PLAIN matter I want to discuss is responsibility for education—education at the elementary and secondary level; education at the college and university level; and finally, education *period*. Who's in charge here?

An address before the Governor's Conference on Education, Rutgers—The State University, New Brunswick, New Jersey, April 2, 1966.

# WHO'S IN CHARGE HERE?

AS ONE OF THE OUT-OF-STATERS INVITED BY GOVernor Hughes to address this conference, I have a protected position. I am somewhat like a consulting chef, called in to advise on the preparation of an exotic soup. I can pace the kitchen, delivering weighty and perhaps lyrical pronouncements about *haute cuisine;* I can peer into the cauldron from time to time, frowning in a knowing manner and suggesting the addition of a pinch of salt; and then, just as the final result is ready to be carried in to the diners, I can smile pleasantly, shake hands all around, and get out of town fast.

I do not, in short, bear any responsibility for what happens as a consequence of the wisdom I dispense. Owing to the guarantees of courtesy usually accorded prophets from another country, I know I can expect some applause at the conclusion of my remarks, no matter how outrageous or irrelevant they may sound.

Well, I intend to take full advantage of my position by venturing a few hard comments. We have had too much politeness in American education for decades, and we are paying for our reluctance to talk about plain matters in a plain way.

The plain matter I want to discuss is responsibility for education—education at the elementary and secondary level; education at the college and university level; and finally, education *period*. Who's in charge here?

In parcelling out chores for the republic which they outlined in our Constitution, the founding fathers left education in the hands of the states. They felt that a decentralized system of education would not only protect but would positively encourage a useful diversity of thought. That idea succeeded. We have 50 different systems of public education in the United States, and though they resemble each other to a surprising degree in some respects, they vary sharply in others. For example, they vary sharply in the degree to which they have delegated their responsibility for education to local communities.

Almost every school offers some kind of science instruction. But in many districts, local voters decide through their support for bond issues and levels of taxation whether the local high school will offer physics and biology as well as chemistry. They decide whether the school library, if there is one, will add new books every year, or whether it will have to make do with the *Five-Foot Shelf* donated by the mothers' auxiliary back in 1930. They determine whether the history teacher will have extra time to prepare for class or whether he will have to double as gym instructor. They decide whether the English teacher's class load will allow the effective teaching of writing or not.

Local control of education has given us some remarkably fine elementary and high schools. But it has also given us some abysmally bad ones, and here is where the balance between state responsibility and local control comes in.

New Jersey ranks third in the nation in its expenditures for each student. You have a right to be proud of that record.

But your state government, as distinct from local governments, pays only 21 percent of the cost of education in New Jersey. By that index, it ranks 46th in the nation.

What does that mean?

It means that your state has relatively little control over local education. And if New Jersey is typical of most industrialized states, it suggests that you had better take a hard look at what is going on in local education. For in most American metropolitan areas, the professional and middle classes are leaving the cities for the suburbs. They earn their money downtown, in the midst of noise and smoke. But they take their paychecks home to a bucolic land of well-tended lawns and well-scrubbed kids.

Fair enough; that is their privilege. The trouble is, some kids have to live in that smoke. Some kids have to play in those alleys hung with last year's campaign posters. Some kids have to go to those schools where there aren't enough textbooks to go around and where the sweet young things who graduated from teachers' college last June can hardly wait for the engagement ring that will start *them* on the road to the suburbs.

These are the children who tend to get lost in the statistics— in the educational statistics, anyhow. They will show up later as other numbers: figures on dropouts, figures on unemployment, figures on crime and relief and military service rejection rates.

But in the meantime, they can be hidden in a comforting batch of numbers that indicate average expenditures per classroom and average pupil-teacher ratios. For the averages conceal, rather than disclose, the tragic gaps in quality between our best schools and our worst. Education is not a matter of averages; it is a matter of individual lives.

And it is these individual lives at the bottom of our social ladder that must be the concern of the state, for many local communities are either unwilling or unable to provide them with an adequate education. No matter how many of its functions a state delegates to its local communities, it cannot delegate its obligation to supervise what every locality does with its freedom to support schools.

I am not suggesting that the state must impose a complete economic equality on all its schools, taxing the rich to insure that every school has a kidney-shaped swimming pool because a few suburban schools have them. Nor am I urging that the state should control the curriculum in local schools, dictating every detail of what should be taught.

But I am arguing that the state must determine what minimum of educational quality it will require in every school and that it must tax sufficiently to provide that minimum quality. It must install a kind of academic floor beneath which local schools must not fall. This still leaves to local governments the option of deciding how high its academic ceilings will be, of setting the local tax level high enough to bring school quality up from the state-imposed minimum to the level of excellence that local citizens want for their children.

It will seem to some that in urging a stronger role for the state in education, I am attacking that concept of local freedom which is so deeply rooted in American tradition.

That may be; but in defining the proper relationship between state and locality in education, I believe that we must stop parroting slogans and examine the implications of this freedom we claim to value so highly. In spite of the fact that extending state prerogatives would diminish local freedom, I support that extension. I do not believe that any locality should have the "freedom" to impose a poor education on any of its children because of civic apathy, or out of the dangerous notion that the children of the poor must suffer because their fathers do not make a proportionate contribution to the public purse. Nor do I believe that any locality should be forced to shortchange its children on education because it has not the tax base to assure them a minimum opportunity to develop their abilities. Such so-called local "freedoms" diminish the freedoms of American children to become complete American men and women, and if no one else will speak for them, the state must.

Further, it is increasingly clear, the state must raise a strong voice in any discussion of higher education, too. For the face of higher education is changing with a changing nation. Like it or not, our society is becoming more and more interdependent, and its public agencies must take a hand in planning matters that were once left to private groups.

Planning for higher education is one of these matters. We have outlived the day when we could relax with Adam Smith in the serene conviction that an invisible hand will guide the ship of state through wind and waves to a snug harbor. We cannot assume that rising demand will always produce the proper supply; that somehow or other the philanthropies of wealthy individuals or the zeal of religious bodies will give us colleges and universities where and when we need them.

Inasmuch as New Jersey has come late to really comprehensive planning for public higher education, you have the chance to profit from the experiences of other states. Their successes and errors suggest at least three components of planning higher education.

First, you must decide what range of academic programs you want to offer your college and university students. What will be the future demand in New Jersey for such occupational specialties as agriculture and psychiatry, social work and dentistry? What kinds of professional men will your cities and farms, your industries, schools, and public agencies require 5, 25, and 50 years from now?

Second, what kinds of continuing education should New Jersey offer its citizens? I am thinking here not only of those who have a bachelor's degree but of working adults who do not have a diploma. Many of them would like to pursue studies that will improve their skills or the quality of their personal lives.

Finally, and most important, who is going to guide the development of higher education? We know who runs the public elementary and secondary schools; the state and local districts do it with elected or appointed boards to take policy responsibility. But publicly supported higher education is in many ways a more delicate matter, and no state can abandon its character to the rigidities of legislation or the shifting forces of political circumstance. In raising this matter, I am referring especially to academic freedom.

In 399 B.C., a court in Athens convicted a teacher on a charge of corrupting the morals of the city's young men. The judges gave the teacher a cup of poison to drink, and he drank it. He talked for a while, in those last hours, of friendship, virtue, and wisdom—and then he died.

I do not know the names of any of those Greek judges who passed sentence on the teacher, and I doubt that many scholars of the classics know them. But we all know the name of Socrates, and we all know the name of his student, Plato, who told us how Socrates taught and died.

One of the most irritating things about great teachers is that they do not always say what the people who pay the tuition bills would like them to say. They often produce disturbing ideas; our sons and daughters come home from college and echo sentiments alien to our firesides and the embroidered samplers on the walls. When we ask where they heard such pernicious nonsense, we learn that Dr. So-and-So told them. And the normal reaction—especially if Dr. So-and-So teaches in a tax-supported institution—is to turn the rascal out.

I do not mean to imply that every provocative or irritating faculty member is on that account alone a great teacher. Ph.D.'s are no more exempt from folly or rashness than insurance agents, plumbers, or commissioners of education.

But if we expect our colleges and universities to support and refresh our society, we must guard the right of their faculty members to produce disturbing ideas. We must insulate them from the financial consequences of our irritation. We must realize that the price of maintaining an open society is permitting and even encouraging the criticism of our most cherished beliefs. If we pay our college and university faculties to tell us only what we want to hear, they will quickly learn to tell us only what we already know.

The history of civilization is in large part the story of societies that did not develop the capacity to appraise and alter their own institutions. It is also, in large part, the story of troublemakers like Socrates whose ideas survived the indignation of decent, responsible, substantial men.

Decency is no substitute for intellect. Some professors do not pay their real estate taxes on time; others do not maintain their lawns or barbecue steaks in the backyard on summer evenings. In short, many professors do not do any of the things that popular folklore says a red-blooded American should do, and in consequence we may resent them.

But liking is irrelevant to education; the point is to listen to our scholars, and to protect their ability to speak honestly.

We can give them the necessary protection, first of all, by

establishing citizen groups of trustees or regents or whatever the state chooses to call its custodians of higher education. These people must have the corporate authority for policy decisions, and they must be so appointed that their rotation insulates their decisions from the varying winds of day-to-day controversy.

Secondly, these custodians must have major planning prerogatives so that they can adjust the developing character of public higher education to the economic and social needs of its people with the benefit of long-range perspectives.

A citizens' board with these characteristics would have no difficulty in attracting to its membership persons of the highest caliber.

What I have said so far boils down to two major points. First, some states have given local communities too much authority for setting educational standards, and they should retrieve some of that authority and use it to insure equal access to quality education for all.

Second, states must realize that higher education requires at least as much planning as a new sewer system, and they must learn that learned men—like teenage daughters—must often be taken on faith because they appear beyond hope and have exhausted our charity. Each state needs a responsible, authoritative body especially to govern higher education.

But all this emphasis on the state is to some degree beside the point, for "the state" is an abstraction. Who are the real, live human beings who must make these decisions about education?

You have a governor; you have a state commissioner of education; you have school district superintendents, deans of liberal arts, high school librarians, principals, teachers, and all the other human apparatus of education. One would think that this hierarchy could provide as many decisions about education as any citizen could want.

If decisions were their only job, they could. But it is at once the good fortune and the problem of American education to be part also of a political system. A governor who presses too hard for tax increases runs the risk of being voted out of office. A state university official who defends the right of an unpopular faculty member to speak his mind runs the risk of being appointed out of office. District superintendents, school principals, and teachers must constantly weigh their obligations as educators against their vulnerability as public servants.

The major thing wrong with expecting a political system to do educational work is that most students can't vote. The people who are most directly affected by deficiences in our schools cannot register an effective protest. That leaves protest up to the educators, to those who have the courage and the conscience to speak out against educational neglect and penny-pinching and injustice. And some of the finest are being forced out of office every year, wearied by public apathy, frustrated by the loss of battle after battle, silenced by elected officials who are willing to lead only after they know which direction the voters want them to go.

Educators have no monopoly on wisdom. The public should speak up to educators, demanding good reasons for the actions they advocate. But the public should also speak up *for* educators. They must let their elected representatives in the legislatures and city councils and boards of education know that they support excellence in education; that they know the price of excellence, and that they are willing to pay it with dollars, with votes, with themselves.

That is why so many of you here today are not educators, because in the end it is not the educators but you who are in charge here. You take charge every time you vote down a bond issue or put it over, every time you browbeat a teacher or back him up, every time you try to silence a professor instead of defending his right to say unpleasant things, every time you grasp or neglect an opportunity for your state to move vigorously into greater responsibility for the planning and financing of education.

This conference offers you the opportunity to take charge at a critical moment for education in your state. It was called to stress the fact that fine schools and excellent colleges do not come cheap—and to find out how much the citizens of your state are willing to pay to get them.

I hope you will agree that New Jersey deserves the best.

# CHAPTER 4

# NEW LIFE FOR THE DODO

THE STORY of survival is the story of
creatures who adapted to changes in
their environment, not of those who
merely objected to change. The dodo
had no control over his lack of ability
to survive. School boards do.

From an address before the Annual Convention of the National School Boards
Association in Minneapolis, Minnesota, April 24, 1966.

# NEW LIFE FOR THE DODO

IT HAS ALWAYS BEEN CONSIDERED BOTH GRACEFUL
and politic for federal officials to include in their formal addresses
a quotation from the President. Not being one to rock the boat—
especially a boat I am riding in, and especially at salary review
time—I would like to open my remarks with a quote from a
president.

The one I have in mind is Mr. Ora Niffenegger who is president of the school board in Des Moines, Iowa. In a speech to two
local school groups last month, Mr. Niffenegger said that the
growth of federal programs for education threatens to make school
boards "as extinct as the dodo."

But the newspaper summary of Mr. Niffenegger's talk indicated that he was not so much criticizing federal programs as he
was the quality of local educational leadership. He was quoted as
saying:

It is not so much the community's lack of money that has brought
the federal government into our educational setup as it is the lack of
foresight on the part of our community, including the school board
and the school administrators, in failing to sense the educational needs
of our community.

As U.S. Commissioner of Education, I found it almost painfully pleasant to read of a school board president who was criticizing himself, not me. And if Mr. Niffenegger is present today, I
want him to know that we have a staff working overtime to find
every fund application from Des Moines, approve it immediately,
and insist that the city accept twice as much money as it asked for.

Beyond that, I would like to thank Mr. Niffenegger for giving me a way to open my talk. For though I do not agree with his viewpoint, I am sure that it represents a conviction shared by many of you here. As such, it suggests a basic question for opening a dialogue among us. *Do* federal initiatives in education threaten to put local school boards out of business?

It will surprise none of you to hear that my answer is *No*. I believe, on the other hand, that federal programs properly used can inject new life into school boards. Far from wringing the neck of a languishing dodo, they can put new sass and feathers on the old bird and give us a very lively fowl indeed.

By way of backing up what may seem to many a most dubious contention, I would like to analyze first the size and character of the federal investment in education.

This year, Americans will spend about $42 billion on their public and private schools, colleges, and universities. Of this sum, the federal government will contribute about $5.7 billion in direct aid to our schools and colleges, or about 14 percent of our national investment in education.

If we consider only public elementary and secondary schools, we find that the total expenditure this year will be about $25 billion. Of this amount, the local governments will contribute 53 percent, the state governments about 39 percent, and the federal government less than 8 percent.

By either measurement Washington emerges as a very junior partner in our educational enterprise, and local school districts emerge as the senior and controlling partner.

However, I realize that this argument from dollars is not an adequate response to the critics of federal programs, for what alarms them is not so much the size of the federal contribution to education as it is its rapid growth.

In 1956, the U.S. Office of Education had a budget of $166 million. This year, we have about $3.3 billion, a 20-fold increase in one decade. Thus even though the federal share of school expenditures remains proportionately small in relation to funds contributed by local and state governments, its rate of growth far outstrips those of support from other sources. The question might therefore logically be raised: If Washington's investment has increased so rapidly, will it not continue to do so until the federal contribution dominates school budgets?

As a former practicing educator who expects one day to return to a life of virtue, I would share that fear were it not for one factor: Congress and the Administration have carefully prescribed procedures for federal programs to insure that the control of education continues to rest in state and local bodies.

The Elementary and Secondary Education Act of 1965 is probably the best example of these procedures. The intent of Congress is spelled out in Section 604, titled "Federal Control of Education Prohibited." That section reads as follows:

> Nothing contained in this Act shall be construed to authorize any department, agency, officer, or employee of the United States to exercise any direction, supervision, or control over the curriculum, program of instruction, administration, or personnel of any educational institution or school system, or over the selection of library resources, textbooks, or other printed or published instructional materials by any educational institution or school system.

This is the law of the land, and any federal official who tampers with its provisions does so at his peril. Even so, one can bend a law without breaking it; to prevent this possibility, Congress carefully specified how aid provided under the ESEA should be channeled to local school districts. Let us look at those specifications.

The Elementary and Secondary Education Act has five Titles. Of these, Title I—aid to schools in low-income areas—is the largest, with about $765 million of the Act's $959 million total. The U.S. Office of Education divides Title I funds among the states according to their current expenditures for each student and the number of school-age children from low-income families. The Act requires each local school district to devise a plan showing how it intends to spend the money it has applied for.

But note that it is the state education agency, not the U.S. Office of Education, that approves the local plan. The state education agencies have full responsibility for carrying out the purposes of the Act through their approval of local plans.

This rule similarly holds for Title II, which provides funds for school library resources, textbooks, and other instructional materials. Here again, the states decide how large a portion of each state's allocation will go to each local school district.

The major differences in the administration of the first two Titles and that of Title III is that federal allocations go directly to the local school districts. Even in this case, however, the U.S. Office of Education acts on local applications only after they have been submitted to the state departments of education for review and recommendation.

Title IV is the only exception to the rule that ESEA projects must be approved by state departments of education. This arrangement stems from necessity: colleges and universities are expected to play a major role in developing the regional research laboratories financed under Title IV, and these in general are not subject to the state departments of education.

But even in the case of the regional laboratories, federal support will not mean federal control. Title IV amounts to an invitation to scholars and practitioners to band together in a common effort to solve some educational problems. The Office of Education does not tell these regional groups which problems to investigate, nor does it tell them where to look for the answers. It does give them the financial backing to carry out those investigations.

My contention that federal financing need not in any sense hamper freedom in education is borne out by the experience of our universities. Beginning with World War II, American universities have served as an important auxiliary to government laboratories and government activities in fields ranging from defense to air pollution control. Government-financed research increased rapidly after World War II, until today federal and state contracts are an important component of university budgets in every state.

The Massachusetts Institute of Technology, for example, derives fully three-quarters of its revenues from the federal government. The University of California receives more than half of its operating budget from federal contracts and grants. And these institutions are only two of dozens that might be cited.

Yet no one would argue that these universities are not free, proud, and vigorous institutions. They were chosen for government contracts precisely because they were eminent, excellent universities, and they continue to be. Moreover, they continue to be jealous of their rightful prerogatives, yet none of them contends seriously that federal financing limits its independence. If federal aid can contribute to the greatness of American higher education without limiting its freedom and diversity, why can it not foster excellence, freedom, and diversity in our schools?

Finally, we come to Title V, and here is the most obvious repudiation of the argument that the federal government intends to control local education through its control of the purse strings. For Title V provides $17 million this fiscal year to strengthen state departments of education—to help them add staff, to finance experimental projects, or to establish special services for their schools. These funds are in addition to federal aid provided under Title X of the National Defense Education Act to help state departments improve their information-gathering services.

I think you will have to agree that both of these programs of aid to state departments of education would represent an odd way of taking educational control away from the states and localities, if that were the aim of the federal government.

What *is* the aim of the federal government in education?

Broadly speaking, our goal in education is the same as in any other area of our national life: to safeguard the well-being of Americans and improve the quality of their lives in any manner appropriate to the rights and responsibilities of the federal government. In defining these rights and responsibilities, we are guided, of course, by the Constitution.

That document clearly leaves education in the hands of the individual states. Most states, in turn, have allowed independence of action to local school districts. Our practice over the years has strengthened the principle that education is a matter for local control, and the federal government has no intention of altering that arrangement.

But while we are discussing the control of education, it is worth pausing for a moment to consider what the localities and states have done with their control. For the fact is that localism in education gives communities the right to have both bad and good schools, and that right has been liberally exercised in both directions.

One hundred years ago, the disparities in the quality of education between states and between various communities within a state did not seriously affect the quality of our national life. Many Americans were born, lived, and died within a 50-mile radius of their home communities. Their schools reflected their communities, and with varying degrees of excellence prepared their students for adult life in their birthplaces.

But American life has changed dramatically since those pleasant but parochial days. One of every five Americans moves every year. We criss-cross the country as readily as our grandparents would have crossed the county. And this mobility, together with a new importance accorded education, presents the states and localities with a heavy trust.

In brief, we can no longer afford to have bad schools. Not even one. For the child who receives a poor education in one state will quite possibly spend his adult life as the ward of another state. The so-called economies achieved by one state through penny pinching in education are more than compensated for by another state's relief payments, unemployment compensation, and crime rate.

Further, every poorly educated individual represents an expense of another sort. We have lost his abilities. We have no way of knowing what contributions he might have made to our common life if his possibilities had been refined through education.

Here is the other face of local control: the recognition that the right of localities to control schools gives them the heavy and almost sacred obligation of protecting every individual's chance to become all that he might be. And in many American communities, school boards and school administrators have failed to discharge this obligation.

The most conspicuous example is in the area of civil rights. It is 12 years since the Supreme Court ruled that separate educational facilities were of their nature unequal. We know, from educational research and from everyday observation, that segregated schools enforce a sense of inferiority that hampers the individual achievements of millions of American children and adults. And yet, both in the North and in the South, segregated schools still perpetuate human failure and human despair.

That is why the Civil Rights Act of 1964, passed by the elected representatives of the American people, invokes the power of the federal government to advance desegregation in the schools. Local and state education agencies share the failure of our nation to attain genuine equality of opportunity in every aspect of American life.

This federal initiative can indeed be interpreted as a measure of control over the schools. But its far more cogent and important characteristic is that it serves the cause of individual freedom. The fact is that a superficial interpretation of the concept of "local control" can harm individual lives by perpetuating deficiencies in our educational system.

The intent of federal education measures is not to control the schools but to help local and state agencies insure that every school in the United States reaches a minimum of quality. How far each community goes beyond this minimum is a matter of local option, a matter for local school boards and state and local administrators to determine.

Thus the federal government badly needs strong state departments of education and effective local school boards and administrators to make its own programs effective. For no matter how wise we in Washington might consider ourselves to be, we know that we cannot pinpoint educational problems in specific areas with anything like the accuracy that you in the localities can.

We know, to be sure, that cultural deprivation is a problem throughout the country—that children who come from homes in which there is no family tradition of learning do not do as well in school as children from homes in which education is valued. We know that these children usually live in the inner city and the rural slum areas.

But these are generalities. We do not know which specific schools in a district these children attend, nor have we any idea of how to divide funds equitably among schools in sparsely populated rural areas and those in the close-packed city ghettoes. Hence we must depend on local educators and local citizens to make sure that the funds voted by Congress benefit the children they were voted for.

Moreover, even though ESEA funds are for certain specified purposes, rather than for general purposes with local educators determining how the funds are to be used, the various Titles of the Act allow local school districts a great amount of leeway in designing projects.

Here, for example, are some projects approved for ESEA funds just last week: a pilot project in Alameda County, California, to teach blind children to travel alone by means of a kind of dead-reckoning navigation system; an information storage and transmission system in College Station, Texas, that will service classrooms in 23 counties; a "summer school in the woods" in Akron, Ohio, that will take 560 elementary school children out into the city's 3,800 acres of parks for instruction in the natural sciences; a program in Lyons, Illinois, that will send communications specialists into the homes of deaf infants to help mothers communicate with their children at the earliest possible age; a summer program that will bring teacher aides from France, Spain, and Germany to give concentrated foreign language instruction to children in Springfield, Massachusetts; and a project in Macon County, Alabama, that will use a Japanese technique to teach four-year-olds to play musical instruments.

I think one would have to dig rather deeply to find any evidence of federal control in this array of new ideas, every one of them the product of local education groups. Their diversity

certainly contradicts any suggestion that federal funds must lead
to a uniformity of practice in American schools and testifies to
the ingenuity and imagination of local educators and administrators when they have the wherewithal to experiment.

In fact—and this is my thesis—I believe that federal programs offer local school board members more opportunities for
genuine educational leadership than their hometown voters do.
For in my own experience, I have found that the average citizen
who has no direct contact with the schools prefers the tried and
true to the experimental, the risky, or the imaginative. I have
found that they prefer to invest funds in the tangible—the new
addition to the school building, or the air-conditioning system,
or new uniforms for the band or for the football team.

But education is not basically a matter of buildings or air
conditioning or uniforms. It is a matter of what goes on inside
an individual, and the changes that the federal programs are
designed to bring about happen inside people. The physical environment in which education is conducted is important, of course,
but I think you would agree that it is easier to put over a bond
issue for building projects than it is to win public support for a
less obvious, less glamorous, but much more fundamental program such as remedial instruction in reading. And because of
your familiarity with the problems of schools in your localities,
you often know that the children of the voters need improved
counseling services much more than they need a new gymnasium.

This, then, is the burden of my statement: that federal programs place a much heavier responsibility on local school boards
than they have ever borne, rather than taking any of it away.
Further, they offer school boards new possibilities for shaping
an excellence in local education that does not depend on local
financing but only on local need and local imagination.

I hope you will take advantage of these possibilities, even
though you might have designed them differently. Certainly we
have had some problems in working out the new partnership
between local school districts and the state and federal governments. We will continue to have them in the future, and by

soliciting your cooperation in the wise use of federal programs, I do not mean to ward off justified criticism.

For we need local school boards, and we need their criticism almost as much as we need their help. We need to devise better formulas for the intelligent application of federal resources now, and we shall need them even more tomorrow when, I am sure, federal programs for education will be expanded to include general as well as categorical aid. But while this criticism continues, let us put those programs to work for our schools.

The story of survival is the story of creatures who adapted to changes in their environment, not of those who merely objected to change. The dodo had no control over his lack of ability to survive. School boards do.

# EDUCATION'S MOST CRUCIAL ISSUE

A S EDUCATORS, there can be no doubt in our minds that segregated education is inferior education. The wisest minds in our profession have joined the Supreme Court in making that clear. What is sadly lacking is the clear public expression of these facts of our professional life.

From an address before the Founders' Day Convocation, Teachers College, Columbia University, New York City, May 3, 1966.

# EDUCATION'S
# MOST CRUCIAL ISSUE

DURING THE PAST SEVERAL WEEKS, MEMBERS OF my staff and I have been meeting with groups of school officials and political leaders from most of the southern states.

Against a backdrop of considerable press attention—some factual, some darkly speculative—delegations have come to my office in Washington. We, in turn, have traveled to the South.

While we encountered a spark or two of fire in the eyes of some of the southern representatives, the conversations were sincere and wholly useful. It was vital that they be so, for we were discussing what I conceive to be the most critical issue facing American education during the latter part of the twentieth century. I speak of the necessity for eliminating segregation from our schools.

In these particular discussions we focused on the segregation that has by official state policy characterized southern education for the past century and continues to characterize it in large measure even though state laws have changed under federal pressures. But the basic issues involved in racial discrimination in the schools are by no means confined to the South. The effort to eliminate segregated classrooms will stir increasingly intense debate in every section of this country. The decisions we cannot avoid making will test both the patience and the conscience of every citizen. Our achievements and our failures alike will have a significant impact on the national economy, on the quality of country ours will be, and on the individual lives of millions of people here in the United States and in foreign countries as well.

As President Johnson said last Thursday in his message to Congress in which he urged new Civil Rights legislation:

We are engaged in a great adventure—as great as that of the last century when our fathers marched to the Western frontier. Our frontier today is of human beings, not of land. If we are able to open that frontier, to free each child to become the best that is in him to become, our reward—both spiritual and material—will exceed any that we gained a century ago through territorial expansion.

Those of us professionally connected with education thus have a heavy responsibility to our students and to our fellow men. That responsibility is of course not ours alone. Eliminating segregation, in the schools no less than in other institutions, will require close collaboration among every element in the community. Government agencies at the local, state, and federal levels must play their part; and so must city planners, real estate people, architects, civic and political leaders, community groups, and many others.

The call to action must come, however, from within the school itself, and it must come from those of us charged with the conduct of education. The school is where the adults of the next generation now are. We cannot allow these children to grow up with a cast of mind which perpetuates prejudice and which forces our nation into another two or three decades of living with the lie that racially separate education can be equal.

Beyond its implications for the professional educator, I do not think it is too much to say that continued existence of segregated schools—*de jure* and *de facto* alike—would undermine and in time destroy this nation's spirit and vitality. Our citizens have always taken pride in their schools, regarding them as characteristically American. It would be a calloused ego indeed that would remain untouched in face of the fact that an enterprise regarded as characteristically American was in practice unfair.

And unfair is the best that can be said about the situation

confronting the Negro child in the segregated classroom. Every experience he has seems calculated to demonstrate to him that he is inferior and should resign himself to being so. The system singles him out, separating him by color from the best schools and the best teachers. The least is demanded of him; the least is expected from him. The prescribed neighborhood he lives in and the restrictions that shackle the adults he lives with strongly suggest that his is a lost cause. His life at school combines with the rest of his life to make him see himself as a second-class citizen.

Great though our country's riches are, we cannot afford this waste of human lives. Nor can we lightly disregard its effect on the position of the United States in the family of nations. Since World War II, the United States has taken the lead in the pursuit of peace and human rights. We seek to advance freedom and to relieve oppression on all fronts—in a world made up of people some two-thirds of whom are not white. When these people look at the conditions among non-white Americans, they have little interest in the lengthy historical explanation of how second-class citizenship for Negro Americans has come about. More likely they will conclude, to paraphrase Emerson, "What you are speaks so loudly, I cannot hear what you say." And we must therefore ask ourselves how long we can expect world leadership to be accepted from a nation that either cannot or will not put its own house in order.

It is necessary that we comprehend these issues. It is necessary to understand that American education—education offered equally and openly to all, not just to the privileged—is on trial. It is necessary to understand that segregated classrooms are not entirely accidental; it is not wholly by chance that our largest cities are marked by predominantly white and predominantly Negro schools and that this separation of the races is on the increase in our city schools. And whatever decisions we make about maintaining or eliminating these arrangements, it is necessary also to recognize that segregated schools—in the North every bit as much as in the South—violate not only the most revered principles of this nation but also our fundamental law.

That position—particularly as set forth in the U.S. Office of Education's *Revised Statement of Policies for School Desegregation Plans*—has been warmly challenged. Some southern leaders, and they are not without counterparts in the North, contend that our requirements are not only unfair but illegal. By what right, many of them seem to be asking, does the Office of Education interpret "discrimination" (the word used in Title VI of the Civil Rights Act) as being synonymous with "segregation"? Why isn't it legal and just to have segregated schools as long as they are created by the choices of pupils and parents or by the patterns of residence which emerge in portions of a school district?

And thus suddenly the calendar is turned back to 1954 and the Supreme Court's decision in the case of *Brown vs. The Board of Education of Topeka.* In its opinion the Court enunciated "the fundamental principle that racial discrimination in public education is unconstitutional," and the Court went on to say that "All provisions of federal, state, or local law requiring or permitting such discrimination must yield to this principle." The decision ended, you may recall, with these words: "We conclude that in the field of public education the doctrine of 'separate but equal' has no place. Separate educational facilities are inherently unequal."

Fortified by these unequivocal statements—and a host of subsequent District Court decisions spelling out the position in detail—those of us in the U.S. Office of Education are on firm legal ground when we move against the principle of the dual school system in the South, with its tradition of "separate but (theoretically) equal" schools and its segregated faculties. These arrangements were originally established by state and local laws, by formal public policy. The segregation resulting from them is clearly illegal under the Civil Rights Act and under federal court decisions.

But to the north lie quicksands of legal interpretation. No major northern city has had—in recent decades, at least—a law or a public policy officially setting up separate schools for whites and Negroes. Segregation in the northern schools has instead come about for a wide variety of reasons connected primarily with patterns of residence—from real estate covenants, for example, or from the flight of well-heeled families to the suburbs; and most of all, perhaps, from the subtle, insidious, undocumented influence of prejudice which herds the Negro into the city ghetto through economic and social pressures which have no standing in law but which operate as effectively as legal segregation ever did in the South.

The consequence is a clearly discernible pattern of predominantly white and predominantly Negro urban schools that have developed without any clearly official planning or policy; and the further consequence is unequal educational opportunity through segregation in many ways more complete and more severe than that existing in many small southern towns. But this segregation —northern style—is beyond the clear purview of the Civil Rights Act and outside the compass of other clearly established legal remedies as of this time.

We face a similarly imponderable situation even when we get into the realm of official action taken by a school system. There is, for example, the feeder pattern, by which children in elementary schools A, B, C, and D are assigned to East Junior High School; while those in schools W, X, Y, and Z are assigned to West Junior High School. The U.S. Office of Education has received complaints from several cities that these assignments have a peculiar way of making East Junior High School all white and West Junior High School all Negro. But is this what school officials actually intended or is it just a coincidence? Unless intent can be established, it is difficult for the law to reach the problem.

We have received similar complaints about attendance zone boundaries and about faculty assignments. It would be difficult not to suspect that some of the crazy quilt attendance zones to be found are the result of deliberate gerrymandering to produce white or Negro schools, or that predominantly Negro faculties in Negro schools are there by something other than coincidence. But how does one penetrate the hearts and minds of those who drew those boundary lines or assigned those teachers? How does one legally establish their intent?

Office of Education teams have spent many weeks in several northern school districts trying to find the answers—trying to determine how we can successfully proceed. But we are not satisfied with our progress, and it is clear that the end to segregation in the northern schools will not come soon. What is more, we face the danger that in the South, patterns of *de facto* segregation will develop as the old dual school system disappears and as more fortunate white families move to the suburbs of growing cities to avoid integrated schools.

The fact is that although a great deal is being accomplished under the Civil Rights Act, this law is not an ideal instrument for changing *de facto* school segregation through enforcement.

Its imperfections were recently brought to the attention of Congress through two bills—one introduced by Senator Edward Kennedy, the other by Congressman Adam Clayton Powell. Both bills are aimed directly at the problem of segregation in the big cities. Both provide greatly increased financial assistance to school districts that wish to undertake programs to alleviate their problems. One of the bills would apply sanctions against districts that remain segregated.

Whatever the fate of these proposals, programs enacted into law by Congress during the past few years are proving their usefulness in helping to make equal educational opportunity a reality for every child. Under Title IV of the Civil Rights Act, for example, hundreds of teachers are receiving special training—at institutes, financed by Title IV—in how to deal with the problems of integration effectively and smoothly. As experience has demonstrated, desegregation means a great deal more than simply eliminating separate schools. There are deep educational and psychological needs to be met, and teachers dealing with newly integrated classrooms must know how to meet them. One doesn't hear much about Title IV, but it seems to me a particularly valuable and important teacher-training enterprise. I wish it were larger and more widely used.

A considerably broader program is at work today in every state and in nearly every community across the nation under Title I of the Elementary and Secondary Education Act of 1965. This Title, you may recall, supports a billion-dollar-a-year drive to bring an array of special new educational programs to the children of poverty—the children (a large proportion of them Negro, of course) whose home and school deprivations are most poignantly acute. The program is working, too, on the minds of school administrators across the nation. It is showing them that poverty is a problem in education and that education is the best way to destroy poverty. And perhaps it is making some of them speculate that the sentencing of Negroes to poverty may be caused as much as anything else by the attitudes of white people.

Closely allied in spirit with Title I of the Elementary and Secondary Education Act is a very special program we are just now trying to get off the ground—the National Teacher Corps. Carefully selected teams of teacher-interns, led by experienced career teachers, will—at the invitation of local school systems—take their dedication and their talent and spirit into classrooms in city slums and poverty-stricken rural areas. It would be difficult to think of a more challenging or more rewarding or more necessary undertaking. I would hope that the alumni of Teachers College would be well represented among the National Teacher Corps volunteers.

All in all, there are about 100 major programs carried out by the U.S. Office of Education. Every one of them, at every level of training, has an important contribution to make to the quality of American education and to making education equally available to every citizen, without regard to race or circumstance.

At the same time, local efforts of a variety of kinds are also whittling away at the issue of *de facto* segregation. Open enrollment programs give children and parents the opportunity to desegregate themselves; the "pairing" of schools that have traditionally been white and Negro is a device with some usefulness in the fringes of the Negro ghetto; busing of pupils to create racial balance is highly controversial but must be conceded to be helpful in some situations; forward-looking schools in many all-white suburbs have attempted to make a contribution through student and teacher exchanges of various kinds.

But all of these laudable efforts, both federal and local, are doomed to failure unless they are fortified by further energies directed at the basic problem.

The first priority is to make sure that the schools which serve our neediest citizens are at the very least equal to the schools that serve our most fortunate. In spite of local, state, and federal efforts, this is not now the case. Buildings are older, teachers are less experienced and not as well trained, the turnover of staff is higher, and in many cases equipment, books, and special services are less adequate in those schools where the child has special handicaps to overcome. It seems to me imperative that while we are forging legal and policy weapons to attack *de facto* segregation in the cities, we must at the same time take immediate steps to bring real excellence to the segregated schools which do in fact exist. The federal government can contribute by establishing programs like Title I of ESEA, and I would hope that my office can bring forward even more adventurous enterprises in the years ahead. But as we do so, we will have to be supported by local resolution to regard the problem as crucial and to bend every effort to solve it.

Here are some things which ought to happen locally:

1. Personnel assignment policies adopted both by school systems and by teacher organizations should be adjusted to guarantee slum schools their share of experienced, able teachers and to cut down staff turnover in these schools.

2. Building programs for the future should be planned so that new schools break up rather than continue segregation. The U.S. Office of Education will provide federal planning funds for such efforts right now, and if I have my way about it we will provide construction funds before long. Moreover, with the creation of the new Department of Housing and Urban Development, there is a new federal tool to help education in the attack

on *de facto* segregation. Planning for new land use and for housing patterns in the city must go hand in hand with planning for education.

3. The next generation of citizens should not graduate from our high schools without having confronted—through serious study and in depth—the issues which confront this society in the realm of segregation and civil rights. Efforts to get this subject into the classroom must originate with states and localities, for we cannot and should not set curriculum from the U.S. Office of Education. But we can provide research funds to start responsible efforts on curriculum development, so that 18-year-olds are not entering adult life without an understanding of the stresses and problems of this society. It is about time we stopped offering an antiseptic history of our country—cleaned up to please the local power structure—and it is about time, also, that we started talking realities with young adults who are joining the military service and entering matrimony at the age of 18.

4. Local school districts must provide in slum schools all of the special opportunity programs found elsewhere in the school system so as to create both the opportunity and the expectation of performance by the children of the poor. There is a danger, well documented by Kenneth Clark in his book *Dark Ghetto,* that our focus on the culturally deprived will result in an assumption that poor children have less promise than others and should be given a kind of special propping up to atone for their status without giving them the advantage of the stimulation that comes from a rigorous educational program. In addition to more remedial reading and more preschool programs, we need more advanced placement in the schools of the slums.

5. Teacher education programs must affiliate with slum schools for their practice teaching in a way to give us many more young teachers who are willing to venture "Up the Down Staircase." And most schools of education can learn from Columbia Teachers College in this respect.

These are some of the tools available to us to help make equal educational opportunity a fact of American life. But in the long run we shall overcome, not just because of laws prohibiting discrimination in the schools or educational programs to dissolve it but because America *wants* us to overcome. There is a new spirit abroad in this nation and a refreshing new attitude. Spreading in large part from campuses such as this one, there is new determination that we cannot and will not divorce such principles as "equal justice under law" from life as we live it.

This determination inevitably focuses on situations where injustice is most apparent, and injustice is nowhere more apparent than in the segregated classroom. Discrimination will not be eliminated from our schools easily or soon, but the course is in my opinion inalterably set.

The changing tide is traced by the results of opinion polls entered into the record of last summer's White House Conference on Education. One of the polls involved the question, "Do you think white students and Negro students should go to the same schools?" In 1942, 40 percent of white Northerners answered, "same schools." By 1963, that figure had climbed to 73 percent. During the same period, the ratio of white Southerners saying "same schools" climbed from 2 percent in 1942 to 34 percent in 1963. Over-all, in 1963, 63 percent of the white people sampled felt that whites and Negroes should attend the same schools. As Professor Thomas F. Pettigrew, one of the Conference consultants observed, "White opinions on school desegregation have undergone extremely significant alterations throughout the country in recent years—far greater alterations than commonly recognized."

It is high time that these alterations be reflected in official school policy. American education must catch up with American life and American law. The citizens of this nation demand that it do so, and they look to teachers and principals and superintendents to lead the way.

As educators, there can be no doubt in our minds that segregated education is inferior education. The wisest minds in our profession have joined the Supreme Court in making that clear. What is sadly lacking is the clear public expression of these

facts of our professional life. The educator must speak out and
he must act. He must help parents understand that all-white
and all-Negro schools harm both races. He must exercise his
responsibilities for leadership, forthrightly challenging those who
would deny the constitutional requirement of equal educational
opportunity for all.

In the face of this most crucial issue in American education,
the professional educator cannot remain silent.

# CHAPTER 6

## THE CITY IS A TEACHER

B UT THE metropolis teaches a different lesson to those who sit in the back of the room. Removed from the scenes of splendor, excitement, and romance that beguile the rest of us, they see only the squalid, the depressing, and the dangerous. And they conclude—rightly —that the city is a prison.

From an address before the City Club of Chicago's annual Civic Assembly, Chicago Bar Association, Chicago, Illinois, May 13, 1966.

# THE CITY IS A TEACHER

THE CITY IS A TEACHER, PLUTARCH SAID, AND EVERY-
one who has lived in a city knows why. Within its few square
miles of glass, steel, and concrete are concentrated the greatest
works of commerce, art, government, and entertainment. Its
boundaries—particularly in the case of the American city, with
its roots in a hundred different nations—encircle the cultures of
an astonishing variety of national, religious, and ethnic groups.

Each of these facets of a city offers its own lesson. But the
kind of lesson you learn depends on where in the classroom you
sit. To some of us, the metropolis represents excitement, a sense
of being where the action is. The mingled majesty and mystery
to be found in a view of the East River, of Capitol Hill, of
Michigan Avenue or the Golden Gate remind us that despite
the normal quotient of tedium and trial in each of our lives, life
in an urban setting can be exciting.

But the metropolis teaches a different lesson to those who
sit in the back of the room. Removed from the scenes of splendor, excitement, and romance that beguile the rest of us, they
see only the squalid, the depressing, and the dangerous. And
they conclude—rightly—that the city is a prison.

Jane Addams of Chicago's Hull House called these prisoners
"the city's disinherited." They are the Americans who have not
shared in the great American success story—the story that
describes how generations of Irish, of Italians, of Germans, and
of Poles labored, prayed, fought, and hoped until they escaped
from the immigrants' ghettoes to a more generous life.

It is in one way surprising that the Americans in today's ghettoes have not completed the trip to Wilmette or South Shore, LaGrange or Lake Shore Drive, for they arrived in the United States decades before many of the other new Americans who have since been naturalized by our melting pot. I refer, of course, to the American Negro. He was poor, ignorant, and without hope 200 years ago. By modern American standards, he remains poor, ignorant, and without hope today. He was a slave in the South 200 years ago, and he remains a slave to unemployment, to poverty, and to despair in the North today.

I have not come to preach a sermon, for sermons have proven notoriously ineffective in bringing about major changes in society. In any case, I think we must concede that the most effective statements on civil rights in our time have not been made from pulpits but in the streets of Montgomery and Selma, Watts, and a dozen other cities less celebrated in headlines but equally effective as object lessons.

I have come, rather, to discuss the educational aspect of the poverty that flourishes in the inner city; to point out that no matter where you sit in the city's classroom, you pay the tuition for the kind of education it dispenses—and whether that education is good or bad, its cost is very high; and, finally, to discuss some measures for improving education in the city ghetto, whether its residents be white paupers or Negro paupers.

In this message to the Congress urging stronger civil rights legislation, President Johnson pointed out that although segregation takes several forms, it nevertheless exhibits a sociological unity. He said:

It is self-evident that the problems we are struggling with form a complicated chain of discrimination and lost opportunities. Employment is often dependent on education, education on neighborhood schools and housing, housing on income, and income on employment. We have learned by now the folly of looking for any crucial link in the chain that binds the ghetto. All the links—poverty, lack of education, underemployment, and now discrimination in housing —must be attacked together.

I suspect that most white people feel a generalized sympathy with the Negro in his struggle for equality. They may object to some methods used by the civil rights groups, and even favorably disposed whites probably believe—after some spectacular incident—that the Negro is trying to go too far, too fast.

But I suggest that it is a good deal easier to counsel restraint in the attainment of a goal when you have already achieved that goal yourself. Moreover, I believe every white man has a stake in seeing to it that the Negro progresses just as far as he can, just as fast as he can. For, leaving entirely aside the moral issue and restricting myself to pragmatic matters, I would argue that our experience has shown that every one of us pays in a number of ways to maintain the Negro in his subordinate position.

Secretary of Labor Willard Wirtz has estimated that every dropout costs the nation about $1,000 a year while he is unemployed. To this expense must be added the waste of individual talent to the nation and the loss of personal income to the individual. We pay for poor education and for poverty in other ways: in crime rates, in military service rejection rates, in social problems springing as much from lack of dignity, lack of hope, and lack of possibilities for family life as from the flawed human nature which we all share.

And such expenses of spirit and matter diminish, finally, the quality of all our lives as citizens of a city—a modern city, moreover, whose boundaries do not stop at the red lines on the maps. Delinquency draws no lines at Howard Street. The North Shore pays rent on the South Side slums; like it or not, we all help to maintain the chain of poverty that binds the ghetto.

The education link in this chain of social slavery is the segregated, inferior ghetto school. What are some of the characteristics of the ghetto school? Why is it failing in its mission to shape free, responsible, capable adults from children who have the normal statistical potential for brilliance, mediocrity, and failure?

First, the ghetto school is underfinanced. Contrary to our American oversimplification, the public schools are not free. They are paid for with taxes; they depend first of all on the incomes of the community's adults.

The ghetto community simply does not have the funds to support schools as educators know they should be supported. It is for this reason that cities need special financial assistance from the state taxing power and from the federal government.

Further, the children who attend ghetto schools walk in the door suffering from handicaps that do not hinder their counterparts in suburban schools. They come from homes in which their parents read little and write less. Although many of them share the universal culture provided by TV, there is more than a little question of its value, both in content and stimulation.

The educator's jargon for these children is "disadvantaged." The term means that they will start slower than children from middle-class homes and that they will not run as fast. It implies that they will not in all likelihood pursue their educational journey as far, unless they receive special help.

Third, the ghetto schools usually have the least experienced teachers; other things being equal, one's teaching, like one's tennis or golf or five-card stud, improves as you do more of it.

The reason for this situation is not necessarily planned discrimination by the school board. Often it is simply understandable human preference. As a teacher gains tenure through years of service, he frequently gains the right to ask for another assignment. And it is entirely to be expected that a teacher with this choice would want to serve in the more attractive neighborhoods. Hence, year after year the ghetto schools must replace vacancies on their staffs with brand-new graduates from the schools of education. It is fortunate indeed that a hard core of able, experienced teachers have made these schools their life work. We need more of them.

Finally, it is characteristic of the ghetto school that it has little community understanding or support. Why should parents, many of whom are themselves undereducated or even illiterate, understand what their sons and daughters do every day from nine to three? They are incapable of judging the quality of the education their children receive, even if they are interested in doing so. How can they frame their questions? How can they articulate their hopes and doubts?

They cannot, and the ghetto school continues to limp along without the material and spiritual support that has made some suburban Chicago schools the finest in the nation.

Why? Is it because the children who attend New Trier Township High School are natural geniuses, the happy product of superior genes?

Not at all. It is because they attend a school in a community where adults care about education, and where adults pay for education. And meanwhile, twenty miles to the south, the children of poor whites and poor Negroes in the inner-city schools are being trained for lives of dependency because they did not exercise better judgment in their choice of parents.

One of the finest treatments I have seen of the problems of the ghetto school appeared in the May 7 issue of the *New Yorker* magazine. The article was mainly an extended interview with Elliott Shapiro, principal of a public school in central Harlem. Here is one of the things Dr. Shapiro had to say about the relation between a child's innate ability, his academic performance, and his home environment:

> . . . It is *after* the first grade that the great disparities between our children and the children of the middle class start showing up. As our children grow older, their lives get worse and, simultaneously, their responsibilities increase. They have more younger brothers and sisters to take care of, and their mothers are forced to become more distant as *their* problems increase. In the fifth and sixth grades, there are more children of broken families than there are in kindergarten and the first grade. It gets harder and harder for the fathers to find employment that will bring in enough money and will also keep their egos intact. And precisely because the fathers *do* have self-respect, they begin to disappear. I remember that during the Depression a lot of us didn't know what to do with ourselves. The Negro male in a neighborhood like this is in a permanent depression, much worse than anything we went through in the 1930's.

What can be done about the ghetto schools?

The Congress of the United States has already made a major

start. In the last three years alone, it has passed 24 pieces of legislation touching every aspect of education from prekindergarten to postgraduate. One of the most impressive is the Elementary and Secondary Education Act of 1965. Title I of that Act is aimed specifically at schools in low-income areas, whether in the city or rural districts. It pumps a billion dollars a year into special educational programs for the children of poverty. It recognizes what school administrators have always known: poverty and ignorance go together. And it is giving them the resources to break up that sad association.

Closely allied in spirit to Title I is a program that we are just now getting off the ground—the National Teacher Corps. This Corps will be composed of teams of young teacher-interns led by experienced career teachers. At the invitation of local school systems, and under the supervision of local school boards, they will bring their dedication, talent, and spirit into classrooms that can now afford precious little of any of those commodities. At the end of their service in the Teacher Corps, they will be ready for careers among the children of the poor.

All in all, the U.S. Office of Education is responsible for about 100 major programs. But not all the education news is taking place in Washington; there are laudable advances at the local level.

Chicago deserves tremendous credit for absorbing a great inmigration of undereducated and relatively unemployable newcomers. I understand that this city has within it more Mississippi Negroes than Mississippi does. It might well have been stunned by the enormous tasks of housing and educating poor whites and Negroes from the South *without* the tax losses caused by the exodus of middle-class whites.

But Chicago's efforts to serve the children who are harder to serve—and indeed the efforts of other cities in similar circumstances—may well be futile unless every citizen accepts this problem as his own—especially those citizens who, like the members of this group, are in a position to do something about it.

What can you and your city do about it?

First, we must recognize that the ghetto school needs not just as much financial support as the suburban school but much more. We must realize that it must provide special services that were considered educational frills just five years ago—such services as counseling and guidance; small classes; remedial instruction; the latest teaching methods and equipment; psychological, medical, and dental aid.

We must change inner-city schools from nine-to-three-o'clock citadels, where all human life vanishes with the dismissal bell, to highly visible neighborhood resources that teach parents as well as children. The inner-city school must create community where there is no other focal point for a common life and shared interests. We must staff our ghetto schools so that they can remain open from morning to late evening, offering adult instruction in everything from reading to making the most of the shopping dollar.

And in this newly involved institution, we must above all create the opportunity for, and the expectation of, performance by the children of the poor. Cultural disadvantage need not foreshadow poor academic achievement, as Operation Head Start demonstrated. Children sense a school's lower expectations and grow to demand less of themselves because the school demands so little of them. Schools are not custodial. Children are there to learn, not just to be kept off the streets.

Children will learn best if they are taught by specially trained teachers. Beyond expressing our national need for more teachers of every description, we have done little to focus upon a kind of teacher preparation which is necessary to serve the children of the poor. In general, our colleges and universities train teachers for ideal classrooms, and although the classrooms in the slums may be in some cases excellent in their buildings and equipment, their human environment cries out for special attention of every kind.

A share of the guilt for this irrelevant teacher education must be borne by the profession itself. Somehow the idea of service to those who need it most has been obscured by the drive for better teaching salaries and conditions.

Further, city school systems must adopt assignment policies that will guarantee slum schools their share of experienced, able teachers. We must counteract the tendency of experienced teachers to choose more pleasant schools as soon as their years of service entitle them to transfer. We must also change the policies of schools and teacher organizations that tend to confront the slum child with the inexperienced, uncertificated, and impermanent teacher.

In addition to more and better teachers, slum schools need volunteers and paid teacher aides to supplement the work of the fully trained teacher. Added personal attention from adults who really care about the child can do as much as any other service to lift the potentialities of the children of the poor.

These are some of the immediate steps that can be taken to improve the ghetto school. But I believe that more drastic measures will be needed over the long run.

For example, traditional school district boundaries often serve education badly and may have to be changed. New York and New Jersey surrendered state prerogatives to form the Port of New York Authority in the interest of improved transportation. If we can make such concessions for transportation, I suggest that we can make them for education.

We could, for example, alter political boundaries to bring the social, economic, and intellectual strengths of the suburbs to bear on the problems of the city schools. Building programs for the future could be planned so that new schools break up rather than continue segregation of both the racial and economic sort. The U.S. Office of Education will provide federal planning funds for such efforts right now—and, if I have my way, the Office will provide construction funds before long.

We have recently been considering financial support for a comprehensive study of a system of educational parks to be established within the inner city. We visualize each of these centralized school complexes as educational centers that would provide classes ranging from prekindergarten through junior college.

And we are particularly interested in finding one or two

great American cities that are adventurous enough to join us in planning the educational park of the future. These entities will house 20,000 or more pupils and will cut across all geographic, economic, and social boundaries to draw students. While such a park would deny the neighborhood school, it would express the vitality, the imagination, and the cultural mix that every vigorous city exemplifies. Students in such a facility would be attending a genuine city school in the deepest sense, rather than attending a school in one section of the city which is untouched by the broader influences of metropolitan life as a whole.

Altering political boundaries or consolidating the educational facilities of a large city would involve major organizational changes —major educational surgery. But I believe that major surgery is required if we are to liberate the children of the slums.

To reach that goal, we will require money; but money is not enough. We will need teachers; but teachers are not enough. We will need research, and educational research is already giving us new teaching techniques, new methods of evaluating academic progress, and a host of additional helps to educate the slum child. But research is not enough.

What is enough?

Perhaps the answer to that question will emerge only when every American recognizes that educating the slum child, which is one way of breaking the chain of poverty, is in his own immediate, direct interest. This is one of the lessons that your city and all the cities of the United States teach: that, as John Donne said, no man is an island—that his well-being, his safety, the very quality of his life and that of his children are bound up with the lives of countless other men whom he will never know and may never see.

The city is indeed a teacher, and it has been teaching us that the ghetto school perpetuates a poverty, an injustice, and a weakness that daily saps all our lives.

It is time we learned our lesson and put it to use.

*C H A P T E R* 7

# BEAR SOMETHING AWAY

"'THE VIOLENT bear it away," says the Bible. Temper your violence as you must, for life is a tempering process. But do not abandon your young violence entirely, and make sure that you bear something away.

From an address at commencement exercises, Vassar College, Poughkeepsie, New York, June 5, 1966.

# BEAR SOMETHING AWAY

YOU SEE BEFORE YOU A FATHER WHO HAS BEEN TRYing, for nearly 20 years now, to gain the undivided attention of either of his two daughters for more than five minutes at a stretch. Today I have the opportunity to seek the undivided attention of 300 young women for 20 minutes, and the prospect leaves me both pleased and puzzled. I am pleased because I have never lost my interest in young women, whether I am related to them or not. I am puzzled because it seems to me increasingly difficult for persons of one generation to dredge up from their years any useful wisdom to pass on to the following generation.

So many of the absolutes valued by my generation are being questioned today that I wonder what there remains for me to urge without sounding square, unsophisticated, or—worst of all—merely quaint. More than 100 years ago, the Anglican Charles Darwin began his researches into the origins of man. He found, among other things, that he could no longer accept the orthodoxies of the church in which he had been raised, and he ended his life as an agnostic.

Darwin was regarded as a threat to respectability by his Victorian contemporaries, a barbarian from the alien land of scientific observation and precise measurement. It became almost a way of life for clergymen and men of letters in those days to refute his conclusions. And yet today we find some theologians—men with impeccable academic credentials, men of a scholarly turn of mind—claiming that God is dead. And we hear the mass of theologians of every denomination reply that although God is not dead, our notions of him require drastic revision. Our human nature, which seemed in 1940 to unite all men with some fundamental concepts of decency, was revealed five years later—at Auschwitz, at Belsen, at Dachau—to be capable of the most hideous perversions. Some of our young men today fight a war which is not quite a war, while others claim that the ancient and honorable name of patriotism has become a cheap slogan to mask the bankruptcy of a nation's moral sense.

God, man, country—these were the absolutes my classmates held when we graduated from college just before World War II. Not that young people in those days were any more noble than now—it was simply that these three words signified some verities which, for most of us, were beyond question. These verities of 25 years ago are much questioned today, and my generation does not find easily the arguments to answer the new assertions of your generation.

But our answers and arguments are not the point today, and neither is the gulf between the generations that grew up on different sides of World War II and the atomic bomb. Rather than trying to inflict upon you some of my own beliefs, I feel it more pertinent to hope that you will retain after you leave college some of the faith and passion that your own generation has expressed so vividly.

I speak of that sense of personal concern for the quality of our society and for the universal cause of mankind which has found a thousand different voices on a hundred different campuses, from California to the Carolinas, from the Mexican border to the Canadian. Those voices, as you know, have both repudiated and applauded our national policy in Vietnam; they have criticized university administrations, demanding more influence for the student body and more freedom for the faculties; those voices have been heard beyond the walls of the academic community, demanding faster progress toward civil rights, toward peace, toward a fair chance for the less fortunate.

And those voices are having an effect. "Nothing succeeds like

excess," Oscar Wilde once said, and no matter how much the
appropriate authorities deplore student radicalism, there is no
question that student viewpoints are altering our universities,
our social practices, and the intellectual, political, and spiritual
life of our nation.

I do not wish either to endorse or to condemn all the sit-ins,
sit-outs, picketings, and marchings. From my vantage point it
seems that some of the student demonstrations represent your
generation's dissent from the uninteresting and perhaps unuseful
orthodoxies you inherited from my generation. After all, in my
day Harvard and Yale students were expressing their noncon-
formity by swallowing live goldfish; ten years later, students
who felt the adrenalin—or the hormones or whatever rises in
the veins of undergraduates—were seeing how many people
could fit into a telephone booth and developing that new American tradition, the panty raid; today, however, student enthusiasm
is directed to the great public issues of the time, rather than to
trivia. To be sure, deans and public officials are frequently
embarrassed because students don't always concern themselves
with finding tactful means to achieve their ends.

But however much I might differ with some of the methods
involved in the manifestation of what the magazines term
"student unrest," I cannot help but feel that these demonstrations
do testify to an individual sense of responsibility for the vast
world outside the halls of ivy. And that sense, in turn, represents
a great leap forward over the relatively precious and parochial
interests of most undergraduates of my time.

To whatever degree each of you shares that sense of individual responsibility for the commonweal, I would urge you not
to lose it. And because the world beyond the academic community threatens that sense in so many beguiling ways, I would
like to discuss some methods of retaining that feeling of personal
involvement in national concerns and—most important—of
putting it to work. Finally, because abstractions tempt one to
be vague, I will place my remarks in the specific context of the
struggle for racial equality.

I hope that by now each of you has an informed interest in civil rights. I do not say a commitment, or a passion, or even an enthusiasm, for often it is difficult to care about a cause until it somehow touches your life. But in point of fact racial injustice does touch every one of our lives, whether we are aware of the contact or not. It depletes us as a nation because it robs us of the contributions that Negro men and women could make to our common life if their abilities were given as much opportunity to mature as those of white Americans. It robs us as individuals because—by apathy, by inaction, by an ethical sluggishness that keeps us mired in our own concerns—we are tolerating injustice.

It is this ethical aspect of the American racial problem, rather than the economic, that has most motivated student interest, and that is a most heartening sign. The question is: What will happen to that ethical concern after you leave college and head for a job, for marriage, for a family or career or both?

Judging from the experience of the generations that have preceded yours, you will begin to lose that passion for justice which your studies, your teachers, and the college environment have encouraged in you. The often melancholy and tedious necessities of adult life do not impinge upon undergraduates with the force they will later exert. For many college graduates, the True, the Good, and the Beautiful finally take a backseat to mortgage payments, commuter schedules, and patio seminars on the best way to deal with a stubborn case of crabgrass or diaper rash.

Not everything goes, of course; some residue remains of those years when daddy or the National Merit Scholarship Corporation was paying the bills and it was possible to advocate socialism because one's tuition and board bills were promptly taken care of by a capitalist back home. Some tincture of youthful idealism survives the onslaughts of mature conformity—usually in a polite, cocktail-hour sympathy with the plight of depressed masses who are much more appealing because they are not trying to move into one's own neighborhood or marry one's daughter.

I suspect that this decline from the brilliance, heat, and passion of student life to the comfortable glow of genteel suburban liberalism is not only inevitable for most, but necessary. The Gandhis and the Schweitzers are always a tiny minority. Men and women do not live by heroism alone but by the humbler actions of earning a living, taking or being taken in marriage, and by fashioning for themselves and their descendants a slightly better life than their fathers were able to offer.

But a tepid, narrowly circumscribed, unadventurous, uncommitted existence barely deserves to be called human life in any but the most restrictive sense of that term. We ought to aspire to something more, no matter how far we fall short of realizing our intentions.

A thousand thinkers and poets, men of action and men of dreams, have offered formulations of what it is to be human. In groping among my mental souvenirs for those that made a particular impression on me, I recalled especially some lines written by a Justice of the United States Supreme Court, the younger Oliver Wendell Holmes.

"I think," said Holmes, "that as life is action and passion, it is required of a man that he should share the passion and action of his time at peril of being judged not to have lived."

". . . being judged not to have lived." What a heavy sentence to have pronounced upon one's days, especially since the very process of life itself brings every one of us a generous measure of pain and disappointment. How additionally sorrowful it must be to reflect, at the close of one's life, that you might have turned that pain, that effort, to some account.

These are sobering and perhaps even gloomy thoughts to offer on a commencement day. The word *commencement* itself means a beginning, and beginnings are usually joyful events, bright with promise as a new morning or a new year. If I could find it in myself to do so, I would encourage you to aim at the stars, to renew this tired world with your youthful enthusiasm and your high hopes—to echo, in short, the thunderous boosterism that has been popular with graduation speakers who take their texts from Edgar Guest and other vigorous exponents of optimistic oversimplification.

But I cannot in honesty do so, for the world simply is not holding its breath for your arrival on its well-worn doorstep. There are more than 2,500 colleges and universities in the United States, and I would guess that every one of them is launching its own corps of confident young men and women this month. Many of these graduates, it is true, have already concluded that the highest end in life is to join the million dollar insurance round table or get on the ladder that leads to a corporate vice-presidency or to snare a man who will soon be sitting at one or climbing the other.

I wish all of them good luck. Civilization rides on the backs of the middle class, so beware of easy disdain. The status you thereby save may be your own.

But civilization quickens and squares its shoulders at the sight of those few who refuse to pick up the common cadence because they hear a different drummer. Those few, those happy few . . .

The problem is that at the age of 21, with a brand new bachelor's degree in hand, so many of us consider ourselves capable of joining that slender band who, in Stephen Spender's words, ". . . wore at their hearts the fire's center . . . and left the vivid air signed with their honour." The grievous truth is that most of us who would stand on the ramparts of civilization must be satisfied with less.

Genius takes care of itself and needs no urging. It needs a spot of affection now and then, some tea and sympathy, but probably more opposition than praise. So to the geniuses in this graduating class, I simply extend my homage and a polite request that you remain until this observance is formally ended, for your sudden exit right now will disturb the remainder of the proceedings.

But to the rest of you—those who recognize that you will probably not trisect the angle or carry the serum to Bangkok or write the Great American Novel—I would like to point out that one can share the action and passion of his time without making a career of it. It is not necessary for you to build the millennium by 1970; it will be quite worthwhile if you manage to place one stone on top of another so that the generation that follows yours—your sons and daughters, perhaps—will stand three inches higher when they look about to appraise their world.

This is especially true with regard to civil rights, for the great battles remaining to be fought will not be waged in Selma and Watts, Montgomery or Bogalusa. The most enduring and critical victories will have to be won in the quiet communities—in the pleasant neighborhoods in our cities and in the suburbs that ring those cities. The great civil rights demonstrations have made their point, and governments at every level—federal, state, local—are responding with legislation designed to bring the Constitution and the Emancipation Proclamation up to date. Much remains to be done, of course, and perhaps more demonstrations will be needed to spur action. But the task of achieving genuine equality of opportunity throughout the United States will not be completed until the desirability of racial justice is accepted by the polite people as well as by the violent people.

These battles will be won by personnel managers who go beyond employing brilliant Negroes to giving mediocre Negroes the same chance for a job as mediocre whites. They will be won by mothers who look at a first-grade reader and decide that all those white faces in the illustrations do not accurately reflect the world their children live in—and who ask the school superintendent to do something about it. They will be won by white and Negro fathers who recognize that a son's bloody nose may be simply the wholesome product of young male belligerence expressing itself at recess, rather than of a racial incident in an integrated school.

These victories will be won, in short, by the mass of white and Negro Americans who bring to the solution of our most agonizing American dilemma a combination of concern and reason. Emotion is not enough; to it must be joined wit and wisdom and a controlled indignation about continuing injustice. Both indignation and a sense of injustice are difficult to keep lively and under control at the same time. My dentist told me recently that he had a new anesthetic. After taking it, you still feel the pain but it doesn't bother you. On social issues like civil rights, it is important both to feel the pain and to have it bother you.

On such social issues, I urge you to reject anesthetics and to preserve that sensitivity to the pain of others which seems to bother your college generation so much. More to the point, put that pain to work and let it guide you to a mature, intelligent, and vigorous citizenship.

The great deeds of the world are usually performed by those who have sacrificed everything else to a few burning desires. We need such people, and we always will. Unfortunately, the very brilliance of their achievement often convinces the rest of us that anything less than brilliance is not worth our effort.

In this day, in this America, we need quiet heroes who, while going about their nine-to-five business, take time to shape a slightly different world from the one they found. We need suburbanites whose concerns do not stop at the city limits, who recognize that poverty in the inner city diminishes the quality of their own lives. We need parents who will extend their concern for their own children to the children of other parents who cannot struggle effectively against economic or social discrimination. We need men and women who realize that equal opportunity throughout American life will emerge not from the organized civil rights movement alone but also from the words and deeds of unorganized citizens whose only banner is an invisible commitment to justice for all.

I hope you will never forget the ideas and the ideals that four fortunate years in a genuinely excellent college have fostered in you, for you owe your families, your professors, and your society some recompense for the privilege of attending Vassar. I hope that you will make the action and passion of the American fight for racial equality a part of your lives, whether those lives take you into the Peace Corps or the PTA. I hope that you will conclude, as Dylan Thomas did, that no one should "go gentle into that good night."

"The violent bear it away," says the Bible. Temper your violence as you must, for life is a tempering process. But do not abandon your young violence entirely, and make sure that you bear something away.

# CHAPTER 8

# THE 1966 DESEGREGATION GUIDELINES:
# A SITUATION REPORT

T HE INFERENCES any man draws are his own business, and I can do nothing about them. Inaccurate information is another matter, and the issues involved —especially the over-all issue of giving our children the best possible education —are such that I cannot in good conscience stand by and not attempt to set the record straight.

From an address before the Alabama State Advisory Committee, Civil Rights Commission, Birmingham, Alabama, June 11, 1966.

# THE 1966 DESEGREGATION GUIDELINES:
# A SITUATION REPORT

WE MEET TODAY DURING A PERIOD OF CONSIDER-able contention here in Alabama over the issue of desegregating the schools as required by the Civil Rights Act of 1964 and earlier federal court decisions. The controversy has focused on the guidelines for school desegregation issued by the U.S. Office of Education under the Civil Rights Act, and on their alleged illegality.

Judging from the newspaper reports I have seen, many of the positions taken about our guidelines are based on misinformation and on distinctly erroneous inferences. The inferences any man draws are his own business, and I can do nothing about them. Inaccurate information is another matter, and the issues involved—especially the over-all issue of giving our children the best possible education—are such that I cannot in good conscience stand by and not attempt to set the record straight. What I should like to do here today, then, is to review some of the facts and reasoning that lie behind our guidelines and to give a short report about where we stand today and what the shape of the future might be. My hope is that a reasoned discussion of the position the U.S. Office of Education has taken will help local school authorities in Alabama and elsewhere to move into compliance with the law as far as school desegregation is concerned. I would be less than honest if I did not add that Alabama presents a special problem which is apparent in no other state, North or South. For this reason I particularly welcome the opportunity to discuss school desegregation from this platform.

Any such discussion must look back to the school desegregation decisions of the United States Supreme Court of 1954 and 1955. In those decisions the Court ruled that racially separate educational facilities were inherently unequal and therefore unconstitutional. Put another way, the Court said that no matter how splendid a school building might be, if it was reserved for Negro students and staffed by Negro teachers, its continued existence constituted defiance of the law.

As a part of the Supreme Court decisions, lower courts were directed to require school districts to make a prompt and reasonable start toward desegregating the schools. In discharging that responsibility, the courts have in many cases felt it necessary to define what desegregation really means. Thus a recent court opinion stated that, "It is not enough to open the previously all-white school to Negro students who desire to go there while all-Negro schools continue to be maintained as such." Furthermore, the schools have been instructed by the courts to make "an adequate start toward the elimination of race as a basis for the employment and allocation of teachers, administrators, and other personnel."

In short, school authorities have been told by the courts that they may not remain passive; on the contrary, they must take definite, affirmative action to eliminate the dual school system.

In July 1964 the United States Congress gave practical application to this proposition in the following statement from Title VI of the Civil Rights Act:

No person in the United States shall, on the ground of race, color, or national origin, be excluded from participation in, be denied the benefits of, or be subjected to discrimination under any program or activity receiving federal financial assistance.

The Civil Rights Act also called upon individual federal agencies to spell this provision out in regulations covering the programs they administer. Such regulations were issued by the Department of Health, Education, and Welfare and approved by the President of the United States. They have the force of law.

Since the responsibility for eliminating segregation ultimately
rests with local school authorities, the U. S. Office of Education
would have been perfectly willing to leave it up to local school
districts to carry out these regulations. In practice, however, local
school authorities raised so many questions or made so little progress that the U. S. Office of Education found it necessary to issue
guidelines establishing minimum desegregation standards.

We issued our first set of guidelines in April 1965. In doing so
we clearly stated that this first attempt to outline the procedures
for school desegregation did not necessarily represent the final
word on the subject, that experience in the school year starting in
September 1965 might very well suggest the need for revision.
This proved to be the case. Even so, the revised 1966 guidelines
issued last March do not introduce a radical departure from the
original document. They do go into some greater detail, and they
call for greater progress. But the original principles remain. The
new guidelines are based on experience with those issued a year
earlier. This experience indicated that in many school districts,
voluntary compliance under free-choice arrangements results in
abuses of the rights of Negro students unless special guarantees
can be provided. The procedures required in the new guidelines
were devised to guarantee that free-choice compliance plans
would in fact provide the student and his family with a free
choice.

I should also like to make it clear that the original guidelines
and the revised 1966 version were not prepared in a quick or
casual fashion. Lawyers for the Department of Health, Education, and Welfare and for the Department of Justice meticulously
studied the law and researched an array of federal court decisions. They agreed that the principles and procedures embraced
in the guidelines were based on firm legal ground found in the
Civil Rights Act, court decisions, and the HEW regulations. I can
assure you that a great deal of competent legal thinking went
into their preparation. Subsequently two court cases have been
filed specifically testing our contention that the Office of Education guidelines accurately reflect the law in all its implications. We

face these court tests with complete confidence. While they are in process, we shall continue with the policies expressed in the guidelines unless a court ruling requires otherwise. I might mention that anyone interested in reading a responsible legal briefing regarding the legality of the guidelines can get a document from us which performs this service.

While engaged in discussing the legal situation, I would like to call your attention to the fact that voluntary compliance plans are one of two ways for a previously segregated school district to meet its obligations under the law. A district which does not comply voluntarily with U.S. Office of Education requirements is subject to court action regarding compliance with the Civil Rights Act. Recent rulings by the federal courts have tended to adopt policies similar to those found in the guidelines for both pupil and faculty desegregation. Right now there is a series of cases before the Fifth Circuit Court reviewing the standards for court-ordered desegregation. We expect that the rulings in these cases will leave scant comfort for those school districts which see court order compliance as the easy way out of meeting their desegregation responsibilities. Any school district which chooses the court order route is, of course, free to do so. Necessarily, however, it will find itself subject to withholding of all federal funds until it can get a court order operating as the result of a suit brought by local complainants.

Summing up this part of the discussion, I should like to make these points:

*First:* The basic issue of desegregating the public schools—of eliminating dual systems of education—is settled. It was unequivocally decided by the Supreme Court in its 1954 and 1955 decisions that such systems are discriminatory and unconstitutional.

*Second:* This principle is clearly supported in the Civil Rights Act by provisions prohibiting federal agencies from disbursing federal funds if there is discrimination because of race, color, or national origin.

*Third:* The fundamental requirements of our guidelines—including faculty desegregation and greater progress in desegregated enrollments—are fully in accord with the law and are based upon court decisions.

*Fourth:* Court orders offer no refuge from the requirements of the guidelines and they involve the likelihood of an interruption in federal payments.

Perhaps it would be worthwhile to elaborate just a bit on the two issues which have caused the most discussion—faculty assignments and school enrollments. Regarding faculty desegregation; it is being said in some quarters that our requirements in the 1966 guidelines appeared out of the blue, without warning and without preparation. Yet those who read the original 1965 guidelines will recall a passage saying that "all desegregation plans shall provide for the desegregation of faculty and staff" and that steps should be taken to eliminate past segregated assignments. Among other things, we required a year ago in the 1965 guidelines that school districts take the first steps toward faculty desegregation at least through joint faculty meetings and in-service training programs.

The 1966 guidelines call for the normal second step. They point out that the pattern of teacher assignments "may not be such that schools are identifiable as intended for students of a particular race" and they look for evidence of real progress toward this objective. Let it be absolutely clear, however, that our 1966 guidelines do *not* require that every school must have a bi-racial faculty by next fall. They do *not* establish a fixed formula for staff desegregation, nor do they tell school administrators what people they may hire and which they may fire. They *do* say this: All personnel decisions—decisions regarding hiring, firing, promotion, demotion, assignment, and reassignment—must be made without regard to race, color, or national origin except to correct past discrimination. And they say there must be real and not merely token progress in staff desegregation.

These requirements for starting faculty desegregation have been challenged as being contrary to that portion of the Civil Rights Act—Section 604 of Title VI—referring to employment practices. We do not believe this to be the case, and we base our position on the advice of our General Counsel. The desegregation process must involve faculty assignments or it simply will be meaningless. The focus of Title VI is on the student, and I cannot imagine that anyone would quarrel with the statement that the existence of an all-Negro faculty in a school clearly signals that this school is intended for Negro students and therefore constitutes the practice of discrimination. Section 604 excludes considerations connected with fair employment practices. However, it does not exclude—on the contrary it covers—the assignment of faculty in terms of the race of the students to be served. In our guidelines we are not talking about fair employment practices. We are talking about eliminating segregated school situations, and that requires the elimination of the practice of making faculty assignments that place Negro teachers in one school and white teachers in another.

As for student enrollments, there are two basic requirements: first, any desegregation plan, of whatever type, must work; and second, in the case of free-choice plans, the choice must indeed be free. In the guideline requirements covering free-choice plans, certain percentages are cited for the transfer of students, the purpose being to give schools a suggested standard for meeting their legal responsibilities to desegregate. These figures have stirred up considerable controversy, apparently based on the notion that they represent arbitrary standards. This is by no means the case. They are simply an effort, based on numerous requests for guidance from local school authorities, to establish broad measures of progress for eliminating the dual school system and to indicate whether or not a free-choice plan is working. Clearly such a plan is not producing desegregation if it continues to maintain Negro schools with all Negro students and white schools with all white students. We need reasonable standards to indicate whether school districts are moving away from discriminatory arrangements of the past.

We must review 1,800 or more plans, and these percentage figures serve in part to help school districts know the dimensions of the progress we hope for and in part to help us decide which plans seem to require immediate attention. If a free-choice plan does not approximate the minimum desegregation according to the percentages listed, that is a signal that we had better take a close look at this plan to determine whether it is operating freely and effectively. The failure to meet a particular percentage does not necessarily indicate the need for a hearing to terminate funds, nor does it by any means suggest that the district should automatically be declared out of compliance on the basis of the figures. It does mean that we will review carefully the processes used by school districts which claim to be operating free-choice plans while still continuing largely segregated schools. In accordance with the guidelines, we will suggest to them additional procedures they may use to achieve compliance.

It has been argued that these percentages constitute an effort to introduce the idea of racial balance into our compliance requirements and that they are, therefore, in conflict with a provision in another section of the Civil Rights Act which prohibits activities "to overcome racial imbalance." This is just not the case. As I have said, and want to repeat, the percentages are an effort to give school officials some guidance as to a reasonable degree of progress that might normally be expected under free-choice plans. Failure to make the indicated progress might suggest —depending on the circumstances—that school officials should take further steps or perhaps that they should change their compliance plan. The guidelines do in fact require that reasonable progress be made, but nowhere do they require that there be any particular proportion of Negro and white children in any particular school. The phrase "correction of racial imbalance" refers to the busing of children from neighborhood schools which have not been officially segregated but which—because of residential patterns—are "racially imbalanced." The U.S. Office of Education guidelines do not bear on this situation at all.

Let me also say this: We are not bent on withholding or deferring funds. Any district that is not in compliance seems to us to represent a defeat. It means failure on our part and failure on the part of those responsible for the schools. Our failure arises from our inability to have helped achieve voluntary compliance under the law of this land. The failure of the schools arises from their determination to cling to a position—a position clearly prohibited under the Constitution of the United States—that threatens the opportunities of children to receive the best possible education. I might add that where such a position is encouraged on a state-wide basis, the result is to create a threat of denial of opportunity to young people which is tragic—tragic in the limitations it imposes on the opportunities of individuals and tragic also because its long-range influence would clearly work to diminish the prosperity and economic opportunities of the state. I might also add that such a position makes it infinitely more difficult for responsible school officials to exercise local initiative in carrying out their responsibilities under the law.

Against this background, let's take a look at where the U.S. Office of Education stands today in its efforts to bring about voluntary compliance. Our basic responsibility, as established by the Congress in Title VI of the Civil Rights Act, has been to insure that federal funds do not flow to any school system which is not making progress in eliminating discrimination based on race, color, or national origin. In carrying out this responsibility we have consistently and persistently sought to secure voluntary compliance with the law. We have made every effort to be cooperative, within the limits of the law. Our policy has been to take action to cut off federal funds only when our efforts have been unsuccessful.

On March 7 of this year we issued the 1966 guidelines and asked that compliance agreements reach us by April 15. Because of the delay in issuing the guidelines, and because of the additional time school boards said they needed to review them and take official action, I subsequently notified chief state school officers that the deadline was extended until May 6. On that date, May 6, we notified state school officials that districts that were not in compliance as evidenced by submission of an acceptable 441–B form should have funds deferred for all new projects proposed under U.S. Office of Education programs.

In addition, on that same day I notified members of the U.S. Office of Education staff that they, too, should halt any action on new projects for districts not in compliance. As a consequence, approximately 100 school districts became ineligible for Office of Education funds for new programs.

In the latter part of April and in early May, we reviewed growing numbers of reports from school districts as to their plans for student enrollments and faculty assignments. These reports reflected what the districts had in mind for the start of school next September.

As of May 6, more than 1,700 districts in the southern states had indicated their intention of coming into voluntary compliance under our guidelines, and we now have received the reports from most of these districts. Many are satisfactory; many are not.

Our first step in the case of districts submitting clearly unsatisfactory reports for faculty desegregation has been to write to the superintendents of the affected schools, calling attention to the shortcomings and asking them to tell us what future action they contemplate regarding faculty assignments.

About 360 of these letters have gone out, and it may very well be necessary to give similar notice to other school districts in the coming weeks. In these letters we sought to make it clear that unless there is further progress in faculty desegregation—beyond that indicated in the first report—these school districts may be called to hearings involving the withholding of all federal funds.

Another activity which has been taking place since the May 6 deadline has been to formally initiate legal proceedings in cases of districts clearly not in compliance—again, toward the possibility of withholding all federal funds. I refer here to districts that have not submitted 441–B forms and that—despite our best efforts to bring about voluntary compliance—have stated their intention not to comply.

As you are perhaps aware from public announcements appearing in the press, we have submitted the names of 18 such school districts to the General Counsel's office so that he may begin the formal processes. The largest number of these districts —six of them—is in Alabama.

I guess we have to assume that similar action will be called for in other cases during the coming weeks. The districts that will be involved first will be those that have specifically stated their determination not to comply. Subsequently, we will have to move against districts that have submitted 441–B forms but in doing so have made it clear that they are unwilling to make reasonable progress in the areas of student and staff desegregation. In these districts which have made some effort, representatives of the U.S. Office of Education will go to the individual school district involved and try to bring about voluntary compliance before getting into the hearing procedure.

I hope that there is no misunderstanding of our position. The Department of Health, Education, and Welfare, and the Office of Education as one of its constituent agencies, are going to adhere to the procedures and policies established in the law. My staff and I regard these matters as our legal responsibility, and we have the full support of Secretary John Gardner in this view. He approves of the requirements we have set forth in the guidelines and of the activities we have devised to enforce them.

We are seeking always to be fair and just, but we are determined also to face up to the issues squarely and to take whatever action the situation calls for. We deeply regret the occasional necessity of curtailing the opportunities of young people by denying federal funds to school districts which refuse to comply. The overriding principle, however, is that federal funds must not be used to support discriminatory practices. In most states there is local effort to cooperate with us in carrying out this policy. I am sure that there is some in Alabama, and I look forward to working with it.

CHAPTER 9

# EDUCATION AND THE
# CHANGING TECHNOLOGY

A MERICAN industry has an unsurpassed history of effectiveness; yet
one of our greatest industries—education—has not fully profited from the
capacities of industry. Forty million consumers of education and their families
await the product of our cooperation.

From an address before the Conference on "Engineering Systems for Education and Training," cosponsored by the Department of Defense, Office of Education, and the National Security Industrial Association, and held at Arlington,
Virginia, June 14, 1966.

# EDUCATION AND THE CHANGING TECHNOLOGY

T HE GREATER THE PACE OF CHANGE IN THE WORLD, the more urgent it becomes for us to develop efficiency in the way our young people learn. This is true because education is a bridge between man and his work; it is a bridge between the present and the future; it is a bridge between what we are and what we may become—as individuals, as a nation, as a world. In reality, the *way* our young people learn to learn determines to a large extent the advances we can make from such elements as capital, natural resources, and trade. It also determines the effectiveness of decisions and actions that affect our national welfare and thus it is interrelated with the responsibilities of the Department of Defense.

As I see it, this conference is more than a regular briefing. On the eve of a major breakthrough in the use of electronic media and their organization into new teaching systems that may change the character of education, we have the opportunity to assess our interrelated roles as partners in shaping the educational tools needed to give momentum, direction, and form to the stream of progress we may have in the years to come.

I should like to go at this subject of efficiency in education from four angles: 1) improving the efficiency in the way young people learn, at whatever age and in whatever subject; 2) improving the effectiveness of programs with vocational implications; 3) raising the incentives and the capabilities of the disadvantaged; and 4) systematic educational improvements throughout the whole educational enterprise—the kind of advancement in education that industry provides for itself through research and development. Actually, research has already played a major part in improving education, but we are now developing the framework for a really systematic research, development, and implementation thrust.

Now, let's look at the first item: the way people learn. Learning is something everybody does for himself, building on his own understandings and needs, at a rate determined by his abilities and his motivations. Throughout our entire educational system, there is the need for individualized instruction. Ideally, each student should have his own personal track. The computer and other newer educational media offer this opportunity. They can bring the best teachers, the most carefully planned curricula, key books and manuscripts to each classroom and to each teacher and pupil. Coupled with the new role of the teacher as an educational diagnostician—as a teacher of thinking and living, not just a transmitter of data—the new approach to learning should keep us from developing a mechanized classroom. In such a situation, the new media can give us a "window on the world," an educational system capable of bringing the best, the most real, and the widest range of experience to the student.

This is important because what takes place in the school is only a small segment of the student's total learning. It should prepare him to cope discriminately with what he can learn elsewhere—from observation, from television, from the myriad of forces about him. Even if we could somehow afford the luxury of a one-to-one teacher-student relationship in school, it would not be realistic preparation for the continuous learning that goes on outside and will continue to go on throughout life.

The new media can do more than extend the scope of what is available to be learned; they can help us to refine the learning process itself. Lately, there has been much discussion about the use of computers to monitor the medical status of patients. We are approaching a comparable ability to monitor the learning process of children. Via the computer and related equipment, we may be able to determine the child's perceptual capacity, his cognitive style, and the host of other considerations that affect his studies. As a result, the teacher will be able to engage in the individual diagnosis and prescription necessary to help each child *learn to learn* with a kind of efficiency that will enable him to tackle unfamiliar situations with confidence that if he does not know the answer he knows how to go about finding it.

Actually, although this involves individualizing the teacher-learning situation, it also involves much more than this; it involves the whole system which makes this kind of learning possible. In the past, each school building—indeed, each schoolroom—has in many respects been an island. It is now becoming common practice to tie these islands more closely to other islands by computers, closed-circuit television, and a host of related media. This poses a new problem in administration, scheduling, time sharing. It also poses problems of cooperation and coordination between those who develop the "hardware" and those who are responsible for the "software."

Our interest is much broader than the elementary and secondary school system; but the efficiency of whatever we try to do in higher education—or even in adult education—depends to a large extent upon the kind of base we have established in the earlier years. At this point, let's look at the newer technology in relation to our second item: improving programs with vocational implications. In the area of higher education, we face a growth from 4 million students today to approximately 8 million soon after 1970. We need this kind of educational maturity and preparation in our labor market and even more in our evolution toward a better society. Here, again, available teaching resources will require amplification by the new technology so that we may bring the best professors and the best programs to our pursuit of excellence in education.

A major part of this growth in higher education will be what is, in effect, the creation of an entirely new educational system out of the junior or community colleges. Hundreds of these colleges are in various stages of development throughout the nation. They have the potential for bringing higher education opportunities within commuting range of virtually every student in the country. Furthermore, as a result of deliberate cooperative planning with local and area industries, they have the potential for contributing to the education-industry partnership not only for entrance to occupations but also for refresher programs and advanced training as well as for adult retraining as needed. Most of these colleges are new and hence without established traditions. Furthermore, because of their close local and regional ties, they are inclined to have a more pragmatic outlook than some of the older institutions. Also, because they are being established at a rapid rate, they sometimes have difficulty in acquiring experienced staff. All of these elements combine to make community colleges particularly aggressive in investigating the merits of the new technologies.

Perhaps we should note also that higher education is no longer the prerogative of the few who can afford it as a stepping-stone to the professions. As more and more jobs demand a level of intellectual and social maturity beyond that provided by the secondary schools, the higher education portion of our educational enterprise must be shaped to accommodate these demands. The newer media will be particularly helpful to community colleges as they fulfill their unlimited potential in providing for the educational needs of young people and adults.

Let's turn now to our third item: raising the incentives and capabilities of the disadvantaged, one of our most significant, perhaps critical, problems. Already, there is considerable experimental evidence that the newer media are particualrly effective with individuals with all kinds of handicaps, including the disadvantage of a poor, inadequate home.

At this point, I should like to digress and point to a particular problem related to our implementation of Title I of the Elementary and Secondary Education Act, a Title intended primarily to improve the education of the disadvantaged and carrying a Congressional authorization of over $1 billion a year.

The major problem with the implementation of this Title has

resulted from the shortage of staff, particularly shortage of those with special skills for helping the disadvantaged to overcome their problems. As an alternative to hiring additional needed professional staff—or perhaps with a view to the future—local school districts have invested a total of approximately $200 million of these funds in equipment ranging from overhead projectors to complex electronic gear. Yet we are quite uncertain that there is available the associated software, the curricular and related materials, to make this equipment an effective tool for attacking the educational problems of the disadvantaged. Such a state of affairs places the effectiveness, even the reputation, of much of the hardware in jeopardy and certainly limits its value to this very important school population.

I recognize that the development of the needed software is an expensive process and that industry has been reluctant to invest its funds in such development. Perhaps one reason is the difficulty of selling equipment to 26,000 individual school districts. I must confess that in this respect the U.S. Office of Education differs significantly from the Department of Defense. The Department of Defense could see a demonstration of a particularly effective training aid and almost immediately place a large order for the product. On the other hand, no matter how effective an item might seem to members of my staff, the best we could do would be to nod our heads and agree that "It's interesting." Eventually, you would have to sell it to the local school districts.

This problem is not limited to the sale of media. In the U.S. Office of Education we face a similar situation in our attempts to make the local school districts aware of recent developments in all kinds of educational research and innovation. Like you, we can sponsor the research and development, but it is up to the local school district to buy or not to buy the product.

We at the Office of Education think we are now on the threshold of a systematic research and development effort that will help the schools across the nation to increase their own efficiency in improving education. This last of our four items—

systematic educational improvement—is the kind of thing Secretary John Gardner was talking about when he said that instead of giving them cut flowers we should teach them to grow their own plants. I am referring, of course, to our national network of regional educational laboratories. The purpose of these is to assist local school districts in assessing their own educational programs and practices, developing or identifying new methods for their improvement, assessing available educational talents and resources, and actually implementing worthwhile innovations. Many of these laboratories will be investigating the potential of the new media in solving their educational problems. Whenever they are convinced that the equipment does indeed make a significant contribution to the educational function commensurate with its cost, they will develop demonstration projects to encourage local school districts to follow their lead wherever similar educational problems exist. The laboratories will have the technical competence to determine whether the software has been adequately evaluated and will recommend to the local districts those systems which have been proved effective.

This effort of the laboratories is an extension of the research which has been carried on by the U.S. Office of Education for a number of years, but the laboratories take the planning and implementation of the research and development activity out to the schools themselves and thus give the whole effort a practical orientation which we believe will help to speed up and give direction to the entire educational improvement effort. The Office of Education will continue to carry on a wide range of research and development activities—from basic studies in cognitive psychology, through development and evaluation of educational techniques, to the dissemination programs necessary to acquaint local school districts with these efforts.

Traditionally, the Office of Education's extramural research effort has been carried on almost entirely at the universities, with some participation by other nonprofit groups. Recent legislation has made it possible for the Office of Education to contract with profit-making organizations for the conduct of research and development programs. As yet, we have not taken real advantage of this opportunity, but we can identify several areas—job training, for one—where industry has unique capability to contribute to our efforts. In the next few months, the Office of Education will issue requests for specific proposals to industry in certain areas of mutual interest.

Surprisingly enough, recent national studies have shown that communication between industry and education has been particularly ineffective in the area of job training. Vocational and technical training establishments report difficulty in finding out what the future needs of industry actually will be. They report that their best sources of information have been the research and development laboratories of the large corporations, not the personnel departments. For this reason, it may be important for industries themselves to reassess their framework for making their needs known to education.

Perhaps we can sum up this discussion by noting that technological advances can make their greatest contribution to educational improvements if we have a close give-and-take between the "hardware" and the "software" people so that they share understandings and objectives. It is clear, from the many weddings of publishers and electronics firms, that industry is becoming increasingly aware of this need. But this is not enough. The partnership must be extended, also, to all those in industry who depend on the human resource development of the educational enterprise and to all those in education who must somehow get a vision of the future for which our youth are being prepared.

The key word is more than cooperation; it is creative cooperation. We look to industry not only to fulfill our demands and prescriptions but, in the characteristic manner of American industry, to provide innovative and original contributions to the educational process itself. We will have to share problems, tell you of our needs, our pressures, our successes, and our failures. We hope you will do the same. In the past, there has not been enough of this kind of teamwork. The solutions lie not only in engineering but in an understanding of the people of the United States—their tolerances, their goals, and their aspirations for their children and their society.

American industry has an unsurpassed history of effectiveness; yet one of our greatest industries—education—has not fully profited from the capacities of industry. Forty million consumers of education and their families await the product of our cooperation. We can assure its effectiveness if we work together and deal straightaway with the bottlenecks and the communications gaps between us. In the business of education, we may have been slow to educate each other. That, it seems to me, is what this conference is all about—to find a better way to educate each other to our mutual advancement as a society. To the extent we can improve our insights and our procedures, we are building the framework for the best gift one generation can give to another—a truly effective education.

CHAPTER 10

# THE HEAT IN OUR KITCHEN

M ODERATION has a great deal to be
said for it, of course, especially by
the moderates. I am reminded of the
prayer that St. Augustine addressed to
heaven when he was a young man. "Oh
Lord," he said, "make me chaste. But not
yet."

From an address before the School Administrators' Conference sponsored by
the National Urban League and Teachers College of Columbia University, New
York City, June 18, 1966.

# THE HEAT IN OUR KITCHEN

In the letter I received describing this confer-
ence, two topics for discussion were identified: first, the prospects
of obtaining public support for integrated, quality education; second, the feasibility of integrated, quality education.

That agenda has a fine ring to it. The word "feasibility" has
five syllables, thus assuring everyone that this will be an intellectual affair, carried out on a high plane by gentlemen wearing
shirts, ties, suit coats, and perhaps Phi Beta Kappa keys. I was
pleased to receive an invitation to join your company, and I sat
down soon after receiving it to compose some gentlemanly, five-
syllable thoughts.

And then James Meredith was shot down on a road in Mississippi. Paradoxically, I heard of this event just a few minutes after
I left a meeting with Secretary John Gardner, Roy Wilkins of the
NAACP, and a number of civil rights leaders accompanying Mr.
Wilkins. We were discussing our progress in school and hospital
desegregation. And I started to wonder whether civil rights was
any place for a gentlemanly discussion. I am beginning to suspect
that it is not; in any case I have the feeling that those of us who
think of ourselves as gentlemen should either stop pretending that
we care about racial equality, or we should step down from our
air-conditioned podiums and start something definite in the way
of a program. Considering the authority that we gentlemanly education officials have at our command to correct racial injustice in
our schools, I feel that we have accomplished very little so far.

We have, to be sure, gotten a fair amount of newspaper space and published enough committee reports on the inequalities of segregated education to build a paper Tower of Babel. Nothing is safer these days than denouncing bigotry. But I find myself puzzling over which is worse, honest bigotry or well-intentioned timidity.

While we have gone on urging moderation, sweet reason, and bigger and better panel discussions, the schools throughout the nation remain almost as segregated today as they were in 1954 when the Supreme Court decided that racially segregated education was illegal. The small progress that the South has made toward desegregation has been offset by increasing *de facto* segregation in the cities of the North. Since 1954, an entire sub-generation of Negro and white youngsters who started first grade in that year has now graduated from high school—most of them without any classroom experience with the other race. The facts today are that a Negro youngster in an American elementary school has on the national average not much more than 15 percent of his classmates from the majority white groups; in the southern states the figure is nearer to 5 percent. White high school students can expect to have nine out of ten of their classmates from their own white group. The picture does not inspire calm satisfaction.

Moderation has a great deal to be said for it, of course, especially by the moderates. I am reminded of the prayer that St. Augustine addressed to heaven when he was a young man. "Oh Lord," he said, "make me chaste. But not yet."

Our words have urged the nation to desegregate its schools. But our reluctance to act has said even louder, "not yet." Somehow we seem to have been lulled into a blind faith in gradualism, a mindless confidence that some morning, some year, a suddenly transformed electorate will spontaneously and joyously decide that this is the day to integrate America.

Well, it's not going to happen. For a variety of reasons—one or two of them arguable, the rest pure rationalization—the majority of American whites display no likelihood of becoming enthusiastic about school desegregation and the changes it demands in the immediate future. Nevertheless, the law of this land beckons every one of us, calling on us to recognize that desegregating the schools is our legal responsibility, that it will not be easy work, and that it is futile to expect the years to erode those passions that today make the processes of desegregation unpopular. Gradualism—no matter what we call it—has failed, and I think it is fair to say that those who continue to espouse it are fooling themselves and, in many ways, failing our nation.

It seems to me time for school officials to form a third front for racial equality in the United States.

At one end of the civil rights movement today we have the gradualists—both white and Negro—a polite and sometimes sluggish team, deeply respectful of the public and sometimes given to assuring each other that it is possible to make an omelette without breaking eggs. At the other end are the activists, both the non-violent demonstrators and those weary and desperate Americans who have come to feel that violence is the only way to get anything done.

The failure of the gradualists would seem at bottom to be fear—fear of rocking a boat which, no matter how leaky, appears at least to be floating somewhere. The failure of the activists is that while they know in general terms what they want to achieve and are willing to pay a heavy price to obtain it, they have neither the position in society nor the professional's knowledge of the means and importance of advancing racial equality within the framework of law.

School officials have both position and knowledge. Those of us who are professionally engaged in education are charged with setting educational policy within our respective jurisdictions, and we are familiar with a variety of methods that can be used to advance school desegregation. What we have often lacked is a productive commitment.

I say *productive* because for all our recognition of the importance of school desegregation to our society, the fact remains that we have not achieved much of it. I say *commitment* because achieving desegregation does not require fury or breast-beating; it does require something much more important: the recognition that school desegregation must be accomplished, and the determination to do it.

Our task obviously requires an activity more sophisticated than the gritting of our corporate teeth. School officials occupy a curious position somewhere between that of the educational leader and the political leader. But it is apparent that for many administrators, a necessary sensitivity to public opinion has tended so to dilute their sense of responsibility for educational leadership that they have exercised it only after the public parade has already decided which way it wants to go.

This may sound to many educators like an unfair and over-drawn indictment. The record clearly shows that school officials today are making remarkable strides toward improving American education. They are coming up with new ideas and accepting the risk inherent in all experimentation.

But to win public support for such advances as team teaching, modern curriculum, language laboratories, ungraded classrooms, closed-circuit television, and computerized instruction is not enough. We must at the same time desegregate the schools. To do otherwise is to accept the shadow of educational leadership in place of its substance. School desegregation is the single point on which we who call ourselves educational leaders prove that we really are so—or demonstrate that we are merely trying to keep things quiet until we receive our gold watches for a lifetime devoted to the status quo.

The fact is that no matter how hard we try, we will not be able to keep things quiet. A revolution is brewing under our feet, and it is largely up to the schools to determine whether the energies of that revolution can be converted into a new and vigorous source of American progress, or whether their explosion will rip this nation into two societies. We simply cannot wait until dramatic action becomes safe, for at this point it is much less dangerous to make a mistake than to do nothing.

Feeding that revolution is a major shift in American folkways. Today approximately two of every three adult Negroes living

in the North were born and raised in the South. This move has
necessarily had a major impact—often a bewildering impact—
on the individual. In some ways, the life he left in the South
was less segregated than it is in the North. The Negro child
born in the South was, to be sure, raised on the notion that he
would always occupy a subservient position, but it was nevertheless a subservient position within a white society. The young
northern Negro of today's city lives in a black society. He has
few points of contact with whites, and those few, when you
reflect on them, are revealing. He is likely to encounter a white
teacher, a white policeman, and a white merchant. He can pass
his entire adolescence without having to deal with the white
world outside the ghetto, and his ideas of that world are based
on three types: the teacher, often a symbol of boredom and
irrelevance; the policeman, a symbol of authority, if not of re-
pression; and the merchant, often a symbol of white cunning.

And so the young Negro setting forth from the ghetto to
confront this white world expects it is going to misunderstand
him and oppress him, and too often he finds evidence to justify
his fears. It is no wonder that, if he has any spunk and imagination, he rejects the fatalism of his father and decides that it is
the part of a man to change this sorry mess he inherited. And if
it takes violence to change it—well, that's what it takes.

It is this young Negro who must be convinced that the United
States is his home, not his prison, and that it is a country worth
fighting for, not a cage to be fought out of. It may already be
too late to change his mind. But it is not too late to provide
his younger brothers and sisters with a healthier belief, nor
too late to protect white children from the destructive stereotypes that most white adults inherited from their own segregated
education.

What tools have we to demolish the wall which separates our
youngest citizens? How can we prevent them from fearing
each other before they have even met?

You are as familiar as I with some of the ideas that have
been proposed to desegregate the schools: pairing plans that

provide faculty and student exchanges between predominantly white and Negro schools; busing to alter the racial compositions of schools in different parts of a community; educational parks that might have as many as 20,000 students drawn from every racial, economic, and geographic sector of a city; supplementary centers for the special enrichment of education which bring together young people from different sides of the tracks for a common denominator of learning.

In addition, there are a number of federally sponsored programs that offer significant help. Under Title IV of the Civil Rights Act of 1964, for example, the U. S. Office of Education provides financial assistance to school personnel and authorities to deal with the special problems resulting from desegregation. Grants are given to school boards for training teachers and other school personnel, and for the employment of specialists. Training institutes are supported to improve the ability of teachers, supervisors, counselors, and other school personnel to handle desegregation problems.

Since the beginning of the Title IV program in January 1965, applications have been received for funds totaling more than $35,000,000 against available funds amounting to $12,275,000. The Office of Education has been able to support 59 grants amounting to $4,900,000. We have supported 115 institutes in the amount of $6,500,000. More than 7,500 teachers, supervisors, counselors, and principals have benefited from the institute training alone.

Title III of the Elementary and Secondary Education Act of 1965 also authorizes federal aid to school districts to help them plan and carry out new ideas for school desegregation. President Johnson requested a special $5 million fund for this purpose in his message on education this year.

Title I of that same Act has the over-all effect of easing the harmful educational results of school segregation because its entire $959 million is aimed at benefiting those children who have suffered most because of the poverty that usually accompanies racial inequities. These are the estimated 5½ million children from families whose annual income is less than $2,000 a year. Here, too, after-school and summer school projects are providing the opportunity to integrate staff and students in ways that are not possible in the regular school program.

Each of these Acts, together with the 70-odd other programs administered by the U.S. Office of Education, has been given a special thrust by the Civil Rights Act of 1965. Title VI of that Act, as you know, prohibits federal aid to any program of activity that discriminates among its recipients on the basis of race, color, or national origin.

Thus the Civil Rights Act makes of every federal program, whether it be for education, urban development, or water pollution control, a powerful financial tool in the drive against racial inequity. The rationale behind this Act is simple: no desegregation, no federal money.

But though the rationale may be simple, its operation is both frustrating and complex. The nation sees that frustration in the Office of Education's attempts to secure compliance with our school desegregation guidelines in the South. We in the Office of Education see this frustration in an even more acute form in our attempts to define what constitutes racial discrimination in the cities of the North and West, where segregation depends less on stated community policy than upon patterns of residence.

To say this is by no means to say that the Office of Education is caving in on *de facto* segregation—on segregation northern style. It *is* to say that the issues are complicated and subtle, that establishing a clear-cut legal basis on which to take action— and be confident of withstanding any challenge—has required far more investigation and study than we would have preferred. We are not satisfied with our pace. But that dissatisfaction adds up not to retreat but to determination to redouble our enforcement efforts where they are pertinent.

The broad position we must all assume on this matter comprises two parallel and equally important policies. One cannot work without the other. The first is to make the schools of the central city such good schools that they attract people rather than repel them. The second is to use every possible device to include within each school a cross section of the social and economic backgrounds of the metropolis. A student should meet America in his school—not a segregated segment of America. In a city with more Negroes than whites and with a continuing white exodus, the concept of racial balance may be impractical except as an ideal. But keeping our eyes on that ideal can help us to do practical things now to slow the exodus and to provide equal educational opportunity.

Some very practical things are now under way at the instigation of state and local officials acting on their own to make equal educational opportunity a reality—sometimes in the face of community opposition, but sometimes hand in hand with community determination to eradicate a century-old injustice.

The Denver school board, for example, has authorized double sessions at one of its high schools in order to cut class size and reduce pupil-teacher ratios to a point where teachers can use new instructional techniques to best advantage. A special pilot program of compensatory education was provided for, and the administrative staff was instructed to draft plans to bus enough Negro student-volunteers to other schools to achieve better racial balance at a school that was in danger of becoming all-Negro.

Summer programs in Little Rock are fully integrated as to staff and students and are being conducted in formerly all-white schools. In Oregon, Portland's program of saturation services for inner-city schools aims at producing an education program so good that it will reverse the flight of middle-class whites from schools in fringe areas that could be racially balanced.

The St. Paul school system is considering a plan to combine a rapid-transit system with a cluster of four or five 300-acre educational parks that would bring youngsters from the ghetto, from other city schools, and from parochial and suburban schools into central locations for classes ranging from nursery school through junior college. Other cities looking seriously at the possibility of similar educational parks include Philadelphia, Pittsburgh, New York City, and East Orange, New Jersey.

In describing the St. Paul plan, the superintendent, Donald

Dunnan, admitted that the educational park may not be the entire answer to school desegregation. "But," he said, "it is the kind of step that's needed. Everybody has been saying, 'Let's do something.' We are."

And that is the point—to do something.

But let us agree on this: in terms of the magnitude of the task, none of these approaches—not the special arrangements made by the schools nor the programs sponsored by the federal government—is a perfect instrument for doing the job. Yet that is precisely why educators who know both the uses and the limitations of these ideas must act on them, for we must supply in courage and in action what out plans lack in ingenuity. There is no such thing as the perfect way to achieve school desegregation. There is no magic key that will unlock all the doors that private prejudice and public pressure have placed in the way of equal opportunity in education. We must simply bore ahead with the tools we have. And it won't be pleasant, and it won't be quiet, and it would be much nicer if someone else would share the work.

But the job is there to do, and if any of us entered education with the idea that it would be a soft touch, this is as good a time as any to concede that we made a big mistake. There is lots of conversation about local control of the schools; if we really believe in it—and I assure you that I am in that number—we must make it work. We must guide the schools to a continuing freedom while at the same time responding appropriately to calls for national action. Local school districts must not sit on their hands and then bellow about having the reins of educational policy yanked from their fingers.

We are in the midst of a struggle for excellent education for every American youngster, and we must use every likely tool we can devise. Local school administrators must consider such means as redrawing school district boundaries and consolidating with neighboring districts for educational purposes, even though political boundaries may remain unchanged. We cannot wait for mayors and city councils to do the work they hired *us* to do. And sometimes we must do work they don't *want* us to do.

There is no point in waiting for real estate salesmen to get the message from on high and ease our job by selling homes to anyone who wants them. There is no point in our waiting for American corporations to start hiring Negro men as readily as they do light-skinned, well-dressed Negro women. Neither American home salesmen nor American personnel managers have ever insisted that they have a major responsibility for building American democracy. They have never pretended to do anything but their jobs.

American schoolmen, however, have quite properly taken a large share of the credit for establishing national unity and freedom of opportunity. Our predecessors in the classroom helped 20 million European immigrants become Americans, and we haven't stopped bragging about it yet. If we are to retain that pride in our tradition, I think we must recognize that the great achievements of the past are not only a legacy but also a heavy burden. If we want to wear the laurels, we must also carry the load.

The load we must carry is that of irritating a fair percentage of our white constituents, of embarrassing some governors and mayors, of alarming some newspaper publishers, and of enraging suburban taxpayers who, in proportion to their means, are not paying as much for their good schools as paupers in the cities are paying for their bad ones.

And all this means that, finally and most grievously, we must run the risk of being invited to resign. Unless all of us are willing to put our jobs and our integrity on the line, we should admit that American educators are no longer prepared to be the prime movers in American education.

American education today is perhaps the hottest room in our national house. But we picked it out all by ourselves. To paraphrase a metaphor first wrought by President Truman, I would say that we must either adjust ourselves to the heat or let somebody else take over the kitchen.

CHAPTER 11

# A NATION OF AMATEURS

PROFESSIONALS in any field sometimes purchase their depth of knowledge at the expense of breadth. The professional, left unchecked, is liable to become a dictator. A school superintendent is no more exempt from becoming a home-town Hitler than the most pompous and arrogant Babbitt who ever headed a school board.

From an address at the 38th Annual Harvard Summer School Conference on Educational Administration, Cambridge, Massachusetts, July 1966.

# A NATION OF AMATEURS

BOUT SEVEN YEARS AGO, THE ENGLISH SCIENTIST and novelist Sir Charles P. Snow delivered a lecture entitled "The Two Cultures." The burden of the lecture was this: Western intellectual life is rapidly being divided into two camps, one composed of scientists, the other of scholars in the humanities. Each camp, generally speaking, has its own subject matter, its own way of pursuing and evaluating knowledge, and, finally, its own language.

This development of differing ways, means, and ends was probably inevitable; Mendeleev's periodic table of elements offers a different kind of truth than Shakespeare's sonnets. But a serious problem arises for our culture. With the expansion of scientific knowledge and the elaboration of a new, scientific language, the two kinds of scholars will be unable to talk to each other. We are presented with the possibility that there will be no middleman to merge the two kinds of knowledge. Twentieth century man will be left with an ethic based on untested philosophies at one extreme, or, at the other, a slide rule pragmatism wholly uninformed by love, faith, hope, and those other human qualities that have always resisted measurement.

Whatever the validity of this thesis in scholarly circles, it seems to me applicable in a much broader sense to Western society at large. This is the age of the specialist in medicine, in industry, in the humanities—even in football, where we have specialists to kick points-after-touchdown. And it is also the age of the specialist in education.

A century ago our schools had teachers who were not specialists. The colleges and universities had subject specialists, of course, but for the most part, elementary and secondary school teachers were expected to teach everything.

Today we have specialists in the teaching of English, and beyond that the teaching of English as a foreign language; we have specialists in counseling and guidance, physical training, driver training, the education of the gifted as well as of the retarded. We have specialists in educational administration as well as in just plain educating.

This subdivision of the educational endeavor seems to me not only inevitable but on the whole desirable. With the advances in educational research, we are finding better ways to teach. We have come to recognize the handicaps that poverty, whether of the material or emotional kind, imposes on the learner, and we are developing methods to anticipate and overcome those handicaps. We are coming to question the notion that there *is* such a thing as a stupid human being, provided he has the basic physical equipment for learning. We are busily updating the curriculum of our schools to bring it closer to what is being discovered on the frontiers of knowledge, as well as to involve learners in the same kinds of processes which result in discovery.

These are all unqualified gains, and they have been made possible by a heightened knowledge of what education is, by increased study, by the evaluation of experience—in short, by an increasing professionalism and specialization.

But as with Snow's two cultures, increasing specialization in education tends to widen the gap between the educator and the laymen who have traditionally shaped educational policy in the United States. A century ago, educator and layman spoke the same language; in general they agreed on the purposes and methods of education. Their cooperative endeavors produced the remarkable decentralized system of schools which has served this country so well.

Today, it is much more difficult to attain the unanimity of the past. Today, in point of fact, it is more difficult for the two even to converse. Can the traditional division of educational responsibility between layman and educator survive, or have we reached the point where our schools must be run by professionals alone?

The most obvious response is that we have no choice *but* to maintain the traditional arrangement, for it is embodied in our laws and customs. The Constitution, by omitting any mention of education, implicitly leaves it in the hands of the states, and the states have traditionally left large areas of educational policy to local communities. Typically the states have given local responsibility for control of the schools to school boards whose members are rarely educators.

But laws can be changed. Should professional educators try at the state and local levels to revise our educational structure and put professionals exclusively in charge of the schools? Or should they, perhaps, mount programs to capture school boards by placing a large proportion of educators in their memberships?

In my opinion, they should do neither, and I say this for reasons that go deeper than law or custom. The first is the basic human right and responsibility of free men to provide for their children and help shape their future lives. Since life in any meaningful sense is impossible in American society without education, it is clear that a parent's concern for his child's schooling rightfully approaches in degree his provision of food, shelter, and affection.

The second reason is much more difficult to formulate and explain. It amounts to a kind of suspicion of the professional as the ultimate controlling element in any realm. Francis Keppel, my predecessor, apparently irritated a number of teachers and administrators by stating that "Education is too important to be left to educators." The French statesman Talleyrand irritated another class of professionals 150 years earlier by stating that "War is much too serious a matter to be left to soldiers." Although professionals of many kinds—among them, scholars in the physical sciences, in economics, political science, history, and law—have advanced our national ability to wage both war and peace, the ultimate disposition of the fruits of their abilities is left to a President, to Cabinet officers, and to senators and congressmen who by the varied nature of their work must be or become generalists.

It would be superficial to ascribe this preference for the generalist to a suspicion of intellectuals. Although we all know Ph.D's who are intensely parochial, seemingly incapable of viewing life except in terms of their chosen craft or art, we also know men of depth in a special field who can step outside their professional realms and bring to their judgments a surprising variety of insights. Indeed, many such men seem, in a paradoxical way, to have gained greater possibility for broad thinking by looking narrowly at one segment of knowledge. Beside them we can set some other rather unusual men of limited formal education who have somehow developed through experience an amazingly generous vision of human possibility and human limitation.

It seems to me that this reservation of the biggest decisions to nonspecialists in the area of decision stems from an intuitive human sense that every government should have built into it a system of checks and balances, an opposition of powers from which—with a little bit of luck—some sort of human wisdom will emerge. We do not reserve the vote to political scientists; everybody who wants to do so may go down on election day to register his beliefs. And somehow—from this paper balancing of cranks against geniuses, substantial men against ne'er-do-wells—emerges the most stable government in the world.

As T. H. White pointed out in his first *The Making of the President,* no armies march on election day in America; every four years, we Americans elect to preserve or overthrow our government, but the only weapon in this continuing revolution is the pencil that marks the "X." So in the government of American education. Our school system, too, has built into it a system of checks and balances. The ideas of the educator can prevail only if they win the approval of the layman. And this is true at every level: the university president reports to his trustees, the school superintendent to his board, and the U. S. Commissioner of Education to the Congress of the United States.

I know how unsatisfactory this system seems at times. We

all know of instances in which superpatriotic laymen have tried
to protect the virtue of American school children by removing
various books from the curriculum. We all know of school board
meetings at which the most momentous decision made was how
many basketballs to buy the team next year, and we all know
of more grievous decisions that have seriously harmed a particular school system.

Yet no matter how erratic and unproductive a lay-directed
policy system in education may occasionally be, I think we must
recognize that specialization brings its own dangers. Professionals in any field sometimes purchase their depth of knowledge at the expense of breadth. The professional, left unchecked,
is liable to become a dictator. A school superintendent is no
more exempt from becoming a home-town Hitler than the most
pompous and arrogant Babbitt who ever headed a school board.

In short, as Alexander King once said of life in general,
"We're all in this hassle together," and we must make the best
of the educator-layman relationship as it is, rather than trying
to alter it in any drastic fashion. How can we improve that
relationship?

I would say first by trying through better communication to
bridge the gap between the two cultures of the educational
specialist and the layman. And by "communication" I do not
mean more words. I mean better words, better English—plain
English. Recently I read of an educator who, being interviewed
for a school superintendency, told the board that if hired he
would try to establish ". . . a dynamic of ongoing dialogue,
structured and spontaneous," between himself and his staff. I
might buy a used car from such a man, but I certainly wouldn't
want him to teach my children English composition or to
hire the teachers who were going to do so. And  I would question his ability to explain any kind of worthwhile educational
idea to laymen.

Educators have often been accused of developing a poly-
syllabic gibberish intelligible to them alone. I think we must
not dismiss such complaints as minor and unimportant peeves;
language is too closely tied to thought for us to regard our choice

of words as a trivial matter. George Orwell maintained—and I think he made a sound case for his proposition—that the quality of a nation's political debate affects the quality of its politics. Words are not merely the vehicle of thought, they *are* the thought, and an idea poorly expressed by an educator is, quite simply, a poor or garbled idea. At a time when innovations and increased specialization make education more complex, nothing is more important to its healthy growth than simple and direct communication from the professionals who lead it to the laymen who are responsible for it.

Second, we should look for ways to put other kinds of professionalism to work for the schools. In the United States today, it is difficult for an educated man not to become a professional of some sort. In fact, I sometimes feel impelled to question the validity of the word "professional." We have commonly reserved the term for attorneys, doctors, and such other elite fellows as ourselves who have gone through a period of graduate study. But the complexity of our society has surrounded us with men and women whose working experience performs the same function as graduate study. Many of us, in fact, become "professionals," whether in designing rockets to go to the moon or packages to sell more soap, and these new professionals can assist education.

The varied talents in every community—the skills of industrial researchers, business administrators, personnel directors, city planners, bankers, social workers, statisticians, builders, lawyers, and countless others—all touch at one time or another on matters that affect the schools. These persons of varied background and special skills and knowledge are needed in the schools in two different ways. They make up a pool of community leadership from which school board members should come, and they represent abilities which, particularly in large school systems, should be employed directly by the schools in order to carry on their affairs. Public education can use the developed talents of such persons to great advantage, both for its lay governance and for professional services.

It behooves all of us who are educators to seek every avail-

able means of interesting the leaders of each profession in serving as a member of a school board or as a college trustee. It
behooves us also to get rid of some of the prickly requirements
for school system employment so that we can be served directly
by special talents which we are now denied. I recall that a
year or two ago in one of our major cities, a prolonged search
produced the best possible man to take responsibility for managing the multimillion-dollar building program of the schools.
But it turned out that he couldn't be paid because he didn't
have the right degree. We must rid ourselves of this sort of
foolishness.

Third—and this may seem odd to some critics of the Office
of Education—I propose that we take a step toward broader
local control of education by increasing the number of school
boards in the densely populated urban areas. It seems absurd
to me that our large cities, with hundreds of thousands of
school children, should limit the advantage of stimulation from
interested laymen on a school board to a single group of 10 or
15 members. How can a dozen school board members give any
sense of representation and participation to the many neighborhoods of a city differing vastly from each other in their economic
and social makeup? It is worth exploring the notion, as New
York City has, that perhaps our largest cities should have as
many as a dozen school boards, each running a cluster of elementary and secondary schools, and each with a majority
representation of citizens who live in the neighborhood. Such
a system would bring the schools closer to individual citizens.
It would give them a much greater sense of direct participation
in the formulation of school policy. It would give district superintendents a much greater chance to advocate promising new
ideas in education, and it would generate a most productive
variety of experimentation.

Multiple school boards would, of course, create some new
problems of relationship to the over-all board of education, but
with proper fiscal and policy planning these can be solved. Decentralization to gain the advantages of local initiative is the

order of the day in many large businesses; we educators need to take a look at decentralization at the same time that we plan consolidation for those school districts which are too small to make quality education feasible. Perhaps I should add that the U.S. Office of Education is in the midst of a program of decentralization through building up the capabilities of our regional offices.

Fourth, we must welcome and encourage a responsible interest in the schools by laymen who hold no official position except that of citizen. I know that superintendents frequently resent school study groups made up of local busybodies or the occasional self-appointed saviours of either the school curriculum or the local tax rate. But these abuses should not blind us to the growing movement of reasonable citizen interest in education. Worthy organizations at the local, state, and national level express this interest, and we all stand to gain by it when it is well planned and well led.

Finally, I would suggest that we educators change some of our own attitudes toward laymen. The roots of the word itself are instructive: it was first used to distinguish ordained ministers and priests of a religious congregation from the rest of the flock. I suspect we educators sometimes tend to regard ourselves as anointed by a holy oil that confers a unique wisdom upon us, and that we literally regard laymen as a flock: sheep to be herded toward a destination we have picked out.

We have no special pipeline to heaven. We have no ultimate wisdom. At best, we are men who have studied one aspect of human growth and who have some experience in using the schools to encourage learning.

But we are only one group of men in a nation of individuals, and we must remember that this nation was put together not by learned people alone, but by various kinds of people with a common conviction: the conviction that men would wind up with better leaders if they chose them themselves rather than letting the choice be determined by heredity, wealth, or social position.

That proposition has worked, both in government and education. The schools have served well the progress of American society. They have created an adult citizenry whose very differences of opinion and continuing debate attest to the success of our schools in perpetuating the diversity that keeps our freedom young. The concerns many of us have today about the deficiencies of the schools and their lack of adequate service to poor and minority group children are concerns which will be answered best by efforts to enlist the lay governors of our schools in providing the answers. We cannot move ahead in education unless the representatives of the people believe in and support the programs for change.

If we claim that laymen sometimes hamper the advance of the schools, we must also recognize that laymen built and paid for them. And they have done a remarkable job. Considering the sacrifices that citizens who are not educators have made and continue to make on behalf of education, it seems to me more accurate to think of them as amateurs—in the best sense of the word—rather than as laymen. For though both words connote a lack of professional qualification, the word "amateur," in addition, signifies a man who does what he does for the love of it, not for what he can get out of it.

Many of us are professionals at educating, but we are amateurs, or at least laymen, in everything else. Let us recognize our own limitations as specialists, and remember that this is a nation of amateurs. More, let us seek to make the spirit of the amateur our own, for certainly the highest motivation for spending one's life in education is to do it for the love of it.

# CHAPTER 12

# THE REALITIES OF THE LEARNING MARKET

L IKE THE drug for which there is as yet no disease, we now have some machines that can talk but have nothing to say. I would caution the businessman not to venture into hardware unless he is prepared to go all the way into printed materials and programing. Otherwise, he will have created an empty vessel or simply a glorified page turner.

From an address before the American Management Association's First Practicum in Educational Technology, New York City, August 9, 1966.

# THE REALITIES OF THE
# LEARNING MARKET

THE AMERICAN CLASSROOM OF 1980 WILL DIFFER
from the classroom of today. One of the influences which will
account for the difference is the vigorous role which private
business is developing in supplying as well as designing the
equipment, the materials, and the services used by schools and
colleges. If business is going to change education, education will
influence business. And if these two assertions are true, it is important to start a conversation between the two, and to open it
with mutual respect as well as with an awareness of difference.

At the outset, I want to make it clear that I come with no
set of government guidelines, no illustrated, step-by-step, how-
to-do-it manual. The best I can do is offer my views on what
looks promising, try to pinpoint some of the questions that
seem to need answering, and perhaps lift a few rocks under
which snakes may be hiding.

First, the promising aspects. It is encouraging to note that
education and business have been demonstrating increasing
affinity of late, an affinity nicely symbolized by the decision of
the president of the American Stock Exchange to leave business
to go into education, while earlier the president of the New
York Stock Exchange had moved from education into business.

This kind of thing is part of a larger phenomenon—the back-
and-forth movement within different sectors of society of some
of our most vigorous minds, men whose allegiance is not necessarily to any institution or any segment of American society but
who are, rather, committed to the over-all public concern. We

ought to make it easier for people with ideas, men committed to an intellectual concern, to move more freely in and out of government, industry, and education. I think we are headed in that direction.

Functioning in a somewhat similar capacity, although in a different role, are the numerous industry executives who lend their experience and talent to the government's interest in education on a part-time basis. At the U.S. Office of Education alone, we have in the neighborhood of 20 business officials serving on our advisory committees—officials from electronics companies, from the U.S. Chamber of Commerce, from the TV industry, from banking, and from a variety of other fields.

Important as such interchange of talent may be, an even stronger force is pushing education and business together. I speak of the lure of the education market: the beckoning outlet for the new media—the new learning materials—waiting to be produced. As *Fortune* magazine points out in its current issue, hardly a week or month goes by without an announcement from some electronics manufacturer or publishing firm that it is entering the "education market" via merger, acquisition, joint venture, or some other working arrangement.

The reason for these mergers and joint ventures is clear. Americans are now spending close to $50 billion annually on their schools and colleges. And the rustle of all those dollars will get louder every year as more and more people begin their education earlier, continue it longer, and decide to invest more in their children's schooling or have their government do so.

Recent federal legislation—especially the Elementary and Secondary Education Act of 1965 combined with the National Defense Education Act—has brought what amounts to a revolution in the capacity of schools to purchase apparatus and equipment designed to serve learning and teaching—textbooks, programed materials, library books, audiovisual equipment, talking typewriters, and whatever other software or hardware may prove itself serviceable.

At the same time, private industry has now been invited

to participate in federally sponsored programs for educational research heretofore reserved for universities and nonprofit organizations. To date, only a relatively few research contracts have gone to industry, and I must add that our fiscal 1967 budget for unsolicited research is very tight. We hope that in fiscal 1968 we will be in better financial shape to expand our support in selected areas. Certainly research in education needs expansion. We spend, proportionately, 20 times as much on health research, and 60 times as much on defense research.

The fact remains, though, that profit-making organizations are now eligible for support—further evidence of the growing awareness that responsibility for educational advancement, in research or in other aspects of education, need not be the exclusive province of educators operating out of our schools and colleges.

Meanwhile, we in education have come to recognize that schools, in addition to being places of learning, are economic enterprises—that a good school is not an accident but represents a prudent allocation of a community's financial, physical, and human resources; that education, in short, requires intelligent management as well as sound pedagogy.

And so as businessmen move into the education field, I think they will find a much greater interest in and acceptance of their contribution today than would have been the case 25 or even 10 years ago. Educators are becoming aware that few school districts can match the business firm's flexibility and management expertise.

This is not to say that the business firm that enters the education field will find itself waltzing down Easy Street. The path ahead is by no means clear, and the long-range strategy for achieving what education in America needs to become will doubtless bear little resemblance to what education has been in the past.

We know, from research carried on during the last decade or so, that we have barely scratched the surface of man's ability to learn and that there is a vast potential for change at every stage in education—nursery schools, elementary and secondary schools, colleges and universities, adult education, vocational training, and rehabilitation.

What we have seen so far in the production of teaching aids is only a trickle compared with what is likely to come when we find the answers to some very fundamental questions. But let me warn you, the answers must come first. If American education is to be served well, we must probe such problems as these:

• How can we reach the substantial number of students in rural and urban slums who year after year have remained almost untouched by the traditional curriculum or traditional teaching techniques or both?

• How can we find out whether we are teaching the right or wrong things for any given group of youngsters?

• Can those who seem to be learning rather well now learn still more?

• How do we cope with the explosion of knowledge—not only in terms of its multiplicity but in terms of which knowledge is worth the most?

• How do we teach teachers to get through to the unmotivated youngster as effectively as to the highly motivated?

• How can we evaluate and alter school organization?

• How do we go about achieving real understanding of intelligence? Can intelligence be "learned"?

• At what age should education begin? Can parents be given a role in education—by which I mean formal education?

• Will all children need individualized attention in order to learn all they are capable of learning?

• How much should we be involved in the education of people in other countries?

• How can we improve the knowledge and skill of two million teachers in mid-career without seriously interrupting their teaching?

• How can we get the most from the individual student's capacity to teach himself?

It seems clear that technology can help us deal with some of these matters—as a research instrument and in instruction—but how it can and should do so still defies us. The somewhat unhandy fact is that we have to be smarter than the machines in order to figure out what the machines ought to do.

We must remember that much of the hardware which industry has been selling to school systems was originally designed for other purposes. While education stands to gain in the long run from technological advancements, there is little evidence that a tape recorder designed for commercial recording studios has all of the characteristics necessary for an effective language laboratory—or that an entertainment system, such as home TV, is equally effective for instruction. Most certainly, computers designed for business data processing are not ideally suited for computerized classrooms.

Sophisticated computers may eventually help us answer some of education's hard questions, and they will undoubtedly be programed to present conventional subject matter very effectively. The essence of education, however, is beyond the capacity of a machine, and always will be. A computer cannot develop a student's ability to associate effectively with other people. It cannot train a pupil to originate ideas, to present them and defend them against criticism, or to talk confidently before a group. It cannot foster creativity, stimulate thought, encourage experimentation, teach students to analyze.

Nevertheless a very substantial body of teachers fear the new communications devices. They see themselves replaced by machines. But teaching a class has little to do with such a job as running an elevator; education will never ultimately lend itself to self-service operation. No matter how effectively computers are used in the classroom, they do not really teach anything. It is the program that teaches—a program designed by a teacher.

I suspect that the fundamental outcome of educational technology will be to free the teacher from the robot role of standing in front of a classroom presenting routine material. Rather, he will become the source of intellectual stimulus, the leader of discussion groups that cause students to think and probe and express their ideas effectively.

One outcome of this kind of relationship will be a great deal more interaction between individual students and the teacher than can now be provided by the conventional classroom. At present, students receive genuinely personal attention only a small portion of the time. The student in tomorrow's computerized school will probably receive far greater personalized attention and much more interaction with teachers than he now experiences.

If there is any real danger from the onset of technical devices it is the temptation to jump the gun—on the part both of producers and purchasers. As Dean Theodore Sizer of Harvard warns, we have achieved technical devices of great sophistication before we have established the clear ends—much less the materials—for them; we have better teaching machines than programs to feed into them, better educational television equipment than ideas on how to use it.

The greatest fear that responsible firms are reported to express is not that someone may beat them to the market but that some competitor may rush to market too soon and thereby discredit the whole approach.

What we are confronted with is an unfortunate combination of sophisticated machinery and unsophisticated buyers. If there are some companies impatient to sell, there are some consumers equally impatient to purchase what is new, what is conspicuous, what is prestigious.

This combination of fast-buck salesmanship and a schoolman's eagerness to latch on to the latest ideas is becoming painfully real in some school districts. Those of us in the U.S. Office of Education have become aware of some of the dimensions of the problem in connection with Title I of the Elementary and Secondary Education Act, which provides nearly $1 billion for children of the poor.

A background paper prepared for a university seminar on

business and education raises this same problem. I would like to quote just one paragraph regarding fast marketing of new products.

The real question here is not what is new but, rather, how can the new best be used? Unfortunately, our answer to this question has frequently been partial or expedient rather than complete or responsible. For example, the so-called new media—television, teaching machines, and the like—have frequently been prematurely introduced before either adequate content or reliable evaluation has been available. The result has been all too often a wave of hasty enthusiasm for the promise of a new technology or device, followed by a more leisurely repentance when it fails to live up to its billing. Such an outcome is not necessarily the fault of the media or devices involved; it is the natural human desire for quick and easy solutions that leads us to hasty action.

I recognize that many schools are making thoughtful and effective use of the new instruments at the educator's command. But it is important to remember the abuses as well as the responsible uses.

So far, I have been talking about problems faced by educators or by educators and management jointly. Now, I would like to offer some sales advice, based partially on what I have already said.

1. My guess is that the businessman will find the education field difficult to attack in an organized way, because decision making is so highly dispersed. The education system of the United States is not a system at all; it is a non-system. And being such, decisions about what to spend and what to spend it on are not centralized decisions at all. The public schools are managed by some 25,000 operating school boards. Their domains range in size from more than one million pupils down to a dozen. Each board prizes its autonomy and has to be dealt with individually.

To compound the difficulty, decision making within any school system may be obscure or diffuse. For example, each system has its own peculiar ways of handling purchase orders —they could be signed by the teacher, the principal, the business

manager, the superintendent, the school board, the purchasing
agent, or even the mayor. One company analyzed its expenses
in selling a machine to a school system and discovered that it
would have been cheaper to send the machine free of charge
when the first letter of inquiry came in. And if it is your impression that church-related schools have centralized and mono-
lithic management, you are wrong. Although they enroll one-
eighth of all the children of America, they make their decisions,
for the most part, school by school. In any case, the business
firm entering education with a new product will find that costs
of marketing and distribution are high.

2. Product needs in education are complex and must not
be oversimplified. Many a corporation, trying to capitalize on
interest in teaching machines, has produced the hardware without realizing that the most important component of a teaching
machine is what goes into it. Hardware is only the razor—and
Gillette makes its money on the blades. Like the drug for which
there is as yet no disease, we now have some machines that
can talk but have nothing to say. I would caution the businessman not to venture into hardware unless he is prepared to go
all the way into printed materials and programing. Otherwise,
he will have created an empty vessel or simply a glorified page
turner.

3. Education is changing fast. It just won't do to design
for the present. The corporation executive must anticipate the
further development of a significant new trend: the breakup
of self-contained classrooms and the release of children and
teachers from the standard room.

The long-range service of business to education should focus
on the individual child, not on groups of children. Increasingly,
children will get information from inanimate sources, from
things. Teachers, freed of routine fact dispensing, will spend
more of their time discussing with pupils the meaning of facts
acquired elsewhere. They will have more opportunity as well
to confront that much neglected group of one.

In short, the new education just emerging will increase the

child's opportunity to get facts from things and values, subtleties and interpretations from people. The role of the teacher is changing, and the kinds of materials needed are changing accordingly. The ultimate and massive market is not equipment and materials for classes of children, but equipment and materials for individual children learning at their own rates and set free from the lockstep of the standard group. Incidentally, the business firm able to make something that would be useful in a school library is clearly in the wave of the future, for the library is the fastest growing element in the modern school.

4. Education is a growth industry. Lead time is important. When our war effort requires less of the economy, consumption of national energies will increase beyond anything now imagined. It is the one product that a lot of people want that also requires a lot of people in production.

As you ponder the requirements for marketing education materials, you might divide up the various functions this way: developing new devices, programing them, distributing and servicing them, and, finally, training teachers to use them. These four elements are part of every new communications device in the world of education, and what people in education and business must toss back and forth is the question of who has the responsibility for each function.

In the development realm, certainly business has a major part to play. Perhaps some research funds from public sources in education will enter the picture, too. As for programing or developing software, the possibility of quick obsolescence presents real difficulties. My guess is that we will have to give considerable attention to the role of the federal government in making funds available for this purpose if we are to achieve a more imaginative result than the economics of the textbook industry now permits.

It seems to me that distribution and service are primarily up to business. But when it comes to training teachers to use the new approaches to education, school people and business people need to establish some kind of conversation. Right now, the training function is chiefly the concern of education itself, partly through federal financing.

We in the U.S. Office of Education have been giving these matters a great deal of thought. And we conclude, among other things, that the relationships among government and education and industry are not guaranteed to be painless—if for no other reason than because we have two countervailing forces. On the one hand, there is the necessity of avoiding any waste of federal funds being allocated to the nation's schools—a necessity that might suggest some set of national "standards" to help school people appraise the educational value of what industry seeks to sell them. On the other hand, we have a clear-cut conviction —as well as legal proscription—against federal interference in local education. The question is how to assure and encourage efficient use of federal funds and at the same time to deter any inroads on the constitutional rights of states and communities to set up their own education standards.

Not only is it our responsibility to protect the taxpayers from waste, but I conceive it as our obligation, also, to do our best to see that justified unfavorable public reaction against waste and carelessness does not wipe out the bright promise of new learning materials and methods. These materials can do much to help the schools achieve the goal of quality education for all. In its own interest as well as in the interest of education, business is called upon to put its best foot forward.

Right now, I have no specific recommendations or answers to advance. I am not even sure that all the right questions have been asked. I hope that in your sessions you will pursue these matters further, recognizing that you are not likely to come up with the solutions in a short time. The issues are too broad and too complex for that, so broad and so complex that what is really needed is the combined thinking of five principal components—educators, businessmen, foundation officials, state educational leaders, and those of us in federal government who work in the interests of education.

Several possible approaches have been suggested toward

establishing a good relationship between the education market
and the firms in the business of supplying it. One might be the
organization of a sort of educational consumer's union, run by
a nonprofit organization and overseen by a standard-setting
committee representing the five groups most directly involved.
Another might be the establishment of a Committee on Educational Development similar to the Committee on Economic
Development, an agency that would be composed of government, education, and industry representatives but would be independent of all three. Its only allegiance would be to the
American people. I have also heard a proposal—not one I am
prepared to endorse, by the way—for a regulatory arrangement
patterned after that of the Food and Drug Administration. So
far, all such suggestions—having come from off the top of someone's head—remain amorphous. I hope that those most concerned will assemble in the near future to devise a working
agreement.

There is only one observation I would like to add to complete
my remarks. We have been talking about the education market
and about the new cooperation which that market will inevitably develop between schoolmen and businessmen. But there
is another area of necessary cooperation that strikes me as more
important than anything we have discussed. Broadly speaking,
it is the necessity for joint action on critical national problems
which go beyond the separate concerns of education and industry strictly defined.

One of these is the employability of people who now have
neither the training for jobs in which there is a genuine future
nor the opportunity to try for those jobs. We must join in determining how social as well as racial minorities—adult illiterates,
displaced older workers, and school dropouts, as well as Negro,
Puerto Rican, Mexican, and Indian Americans—can be trained
for productive functions that offer the independence and self-
respect necessary to full citizenship in a nation of free men.

We must consider together the cause for the rapid decline
in our central cities and decide how the distinctive knowledge

and abilities of educators and businessmen can arrest an atrophy that threatens the ecnomic, political, and social life of most of our population.

These are some of the matters that will be in our conversation as educators. We hope they will be in yours, for we expect to learn much from you. We hope to improve our executive abilities by observing yours. We hope to improve our management expertise as we benefit from yours. Finally, we hope to improve our salaries by comparing them with yours— and on that scholarly note let me close.

# CHAPTER 13

# PROSE, POETRY, AND BLACK POWER

W E SIT in our secure and unchallenged positions and try to do something about injustice; the Negroes live it every day, and no man—no matter how sympathetic and earnest—can adequately appreciate a suffering he has never experienced. We are all locked in the castles of who we are, barricaded behind our limited lives. We are all culturally deprived.

---

An address before the Annual Convocation of Hampton Institute, Hampton, Virginia, September 29, 1966.

# PROSE, POETRY, AND BLACK POWER

FOR JUST ABOUT 10 YEARS—EVER SINCE ROSA PARKS told a Montgomery bus driver she was too tired to stand up and give her seat to a white passenger—the long, hot summers have stirred increasing strife and apprehension. Driven by old frustrations combined with occasional new successes, the heirs of Rosa Parks' courageous decision have become more assured and outspoken in their demands. Meanwhile, a large portion of the white majority, sometimes seeming to be almost deliberately unaware of the hopelessness that is routine for millions of Negro Americans, has come to look upon civil rights activity as destructive and unwarranted rather than as an expression of fundamental American ideals.

This summer of 1966 has been the longest and hottest of all. And with the opening of schools in some sections of the South during the first weeks of this month, the advent of autumn has not meant closing out our summer of violence—rather, the season has been extended to include additional days of contention in our national calendar.

In any case, we are left to contemplate the simmering hatreds of a dozen communities and to determine how badly damaged is our effort to extend full citizenship to every American. It remains for us also to argue about the course this effort should take in the near future.

I offer an inventory and some suggestions with a good deal of hesitation, for the events of this summer have been both baffling and depressing. The painful, sometimes faltering, progress of our national march toward equal opportunity in education, in work, and in daily living, toward real-life, day-to-day expression of the American ideal for every American, must often tempt many conscientious citizens to despair that we shall ever succeed in removing traditional limitations on the achievement of liberty and justice for all. At such moments it is instructive to recollect the equally erratic journey the people of the United States have made from 1776 until now.

The United States began life as a white, Anglo-Saxon, Protestant country. Its birth was attended by a Scotsman named John Paul Jones, two Poles named Kosciusko and Pulaski, a German named von Steuben, a French admiral named DeGrasse, and a Negro named Crispus Attucks. Nevertheless, when the smoke cleared, we continued to regard ourselves mainly as a nation of transplanted Englishmen.

Then came the Irish and the Germans. If you look at the political cartoons of the day, you will see the Irishman portrayed as a hulking bumpkin with a clay pipe in his mouth, and the German as a pompous martinet with a belly swollen by beer. We have made stereotypes of national minorities in America just as we have done for our racial minorities, be they Indian, Negro, Oriental, or those from some other background. These stereotypes still influence our thinking, although to a diminishing degree, and all of them are false.

The Irish and Germans were followed by the Italians and Poles, thereby enriching our national stock of clichés with organ-grinders, banana vendors, sausage makers, and tackles for the "Fighting Irish" of Notre Dame. And over the years we have seen the struggle for acceptance which has been waged at various times and places by Jews and many others with enough distinctiveness of appearance or culture to make them an identifiable minority.

Not one of these groups was Americanized without fierce effort on its part and fierce resistance on the part of those who preceded them. Those advocates of sweetness and light who believe that the social tranquility of middle-class, white Ameri-

cans flowed serenely and inevitably from the Constitution as
written in 1787 do not know their history. Parts of our populace
have been fighting to achieve freedom and dignity in every
period of our history. And from time to time they have inter-
rupted their battle at home to join hands with their erstwhile
opponents in fighting our national enemies abroad, as Harlem
Negroes are fighting alongside Mississippi whites in Vietnam
today.

So the contemporary Negro fight for justice and equality of
opportunity has plenty of precedents in the American record.
Far from being subversive in its origins, it is essentially American
and essentially true to the spirit of 1776 as well as to the spirit
and the fact of the history which has followed.

But even though the Negro's situation today bears analogies
to the situation of other minorities in other times, his battle
will be much more difficult to win. Negroes bear a much heavier
load of prejudice than any preceding group; and, paradoxically,
they do so in a land where their forebears preceded most of
the ancestors of those who limit the Negro's opportunity. The
upward climb to equality and acceptance has been steeper and
longer for the Negro American; we should not be surprised that
he has occasionally erupted into violence in frustration with the
extra burdens that are placed upon him by the fact of racial
prejudice.

The appalling destruction of Watts may have demonstrated
the dimensions of the burden of frustration which years of denied opportunity can produce. Perhaps Watts taught us something. But what did Atlanta teach us a few weeks ago? That
this southern city, despite its exemplary progress in improving
race relations, still has a long way to go? No sensible white man
doubted that, and no sensible Negro can deny that Atlanta
has done more in the South than many cities in the North to
seek constructive solutions to the perplexing issues of race relations in our society.

All that the recent Atlanta riots proved—and at exorbitant
cost—is this: No single Negro, no single civil rights organization

speaks for all Negroes. Atlanta reminded us of something that many Negroes and whites tend to forget: there *is* no such thing as "the Negro." An identifiable, classifiable racial characteristic cannot conceal all those individual differences of conviction and preference that each of us guards as his own.

A corollary to this proposition is that there is no such thing as "the white man." Mister Charlie is as much a fiction as Uncle Tom. What is in a man's heart is not determined by the color of his skin. You must believe that millions of whites feel as deep a sense of shame about incidents such as Cicero and Grenada as Negroes feel anger and pain and the need for redress of wrong.

I question the ability of white men in comfortable circumstances to say anything perceptive about racial equality to the millions of Negroes who live with a hundred daily frustrations we cannot know. We sit in our secure and unchallenged positions and try to do something about injustice; the Negroes live it every day, and no man—no matter how sympathetic and earnest —can adequately appreciate a suffering he has never experienced. We are all locked in the castles of who we are, barricaded behind our limited lives. We are all culturally deprived. We are all disadvantaged in our ability to comprehend our fellow Americans.

Yet at some point, some of us must try to reach one another. We must try to speak above the passion-generated slogans chanted by the ignorant or the bigoted or the mistaken of both races and say something that probes beneath the usual simplicities about brotherhood.

And at this point in time, speaking to college students, not to prisoners of a ghetto, I must say that every repetition of Watts—whatever awakening function the original might have served—can only strengthen those who would forever exclude the American Negro from the rights he should have inherited at birth. What remains is the essentially more dreary and routine job of converting the energy of passion to constructive action.

As our newspapers report, Mao Tse-tung is finding it difficult to bring all his countrymen to that level of revolutionary ardor *he* apparently experiences daily. Most recently, in an attempt to inject youth and vigor into his flagging Utopia, he has loosed upon his country an army of teenage enthusiasts called the Red Guards. So far, their accomplishment has been to terrify some nuns, rename some streets, and discourage some former friends in other nations. A Russian observer had this to say about Mao's difficulties: "Seizing power is poetry, but running a country is prose. Mao's trouble is that he persists in being a poet."

Every election year, Americans share the boisterous poetry of assuming power. Our election campaigns, as many Europeans have pointed out, tend to have a flamboyant, carnival air about them. Along with the speeches and debates, we have pretty girls wearing red, white, and blue sashes; we have horns, whistles, billboards, bumper stickers, bands, parades, and vast amounts of the noise and bombast that characterize the operation of democracy—American style.

But after all the noise is over and all the confetti has been swept up, the cadre of Americans elected or appointed to office has to buckle down to the serious business of government. And government is only rarely festive; only rarely is it poetry. Government—you find out after you've been in it a while—boils down to the homely business of this desk, these papers, that telephone, and a hundred meetings with other fallible men like yourself who are trying to keep a roof on our national house and maybe rearrange some of the furniture inside to make the place more livable while we try simultaneously to live as good neighbors to the people next door.

Similarly, I would say that the civil rights struggle has passed the poetry phase. Now is the time for prose.

Most of you are Negroes, and as college students you form an elite minority within a minority. The future of black power—however that phrase is ultimately defined—lies with you. Whether the physical, spiritual, and intellectual energies of 20 million Negroes swell our national resources or deplete them depends to a high degree on Negro leadership that is at once educated and responsible.

I am not urging you to acquiesce in injustice. I am not asking you to quiet down and stop insisting on your rights as American citizens. I *am* urging on you the painful recognition that the Negro will win full citizenship in the same way that other American minorities have won it: not by blasting through closed doors in a few explosive moments but by shoving those doors back inch by inch until the rust on our social hinges gives way.

There may be those who will think it unfair to ask Negroes to accept a program of persistent, lawful aggressiveness. They will argue that the denial of rights for more than a century of freedom—freedom in name but not in fact—justifies any measure to grasp freedom, even if it means seeking power through separation from white America.

But fairness is not the only issue. Perhaps equally important is how best to achieve what unfairness has denied. As we move through our lives, each of us must answer for himself the question: How does a man best oppose injustice?

Negroes have been urged to seek "black power." Black power can be a useful concept *if* it is defined as demanding a rightful place for the Negro American in our national sun; gaining political influence so that the Negro as an individual has a proper say in the affairs of a nation which his suffering and exploitation helped build; winning, above all, that sense of self-respect and personal dignity which has been denied him.

But no thoughtful American with a knowledge of our history and traditions can endorse a concept of black power that encourages separatism. You must defeat injustice, not retreat from it to a racial unity that, while offering a spurious comfort, brings with it national division. A ghetto is a ghetto, whether it be bounded by a few city blocks or a large portion of a nation. The object is to knock down the barriers, not to shelter behind their doubtful security.

And a major part of the effort to remove those barriers will fall to college-educated Negroes more so than to those who are tired of patience and seek any outlet for their anger because they are trapped in their own understandable frustrations. You must do what they cannot do: you must show that it is possible to take your place in American society through your talent and your ability. You must use your intellect and achievement to circumvent injustice when you cannot drive straight through it.

You must compete with the white man in his own arena: his corporations, his government, his universities. You must walk the same weary road that the Irish and Italians and Jews walked before you. And regardless of how much opposition you meet on that road from whites, no matter how much jeering you hear from Negroes on the sidelines, you must keep coming. The place you're headed for is worth getting to, for you and for your sons and for theirs.

The power which will make it possible for you to walk this road successfully will come from high quality education. Until recent years, any Negro had a right to be cynical about anyone's urging him to seek a college education. So many opportunities in industry, in government, and in all phases of private and public life were closed to him that it did not seem to make much difference whether he was educated or not.

But today it *does* make a difference, and today that former cynicism must give way to a sense of urgency. Our entire economy has changed rapidly from one depending heavily on sheer manpower with a sprinkling of technicians and managers on top to one that requires a large percentage of highly trained and well-educated people. The old aristocracies of family, social connections, and inherited wealth are giving way to a new aristocracy of intellect and imagination. The future lies not in white power or black power but in brain power, pure and simple.

The new importance of education in economic, scientific, and political endeavor is forcing us to reexamine the effectiveness of our schools, and this reexamination has already brought change from first grade through graduate school. It has helped Negro Americans appreciate the importance of the schools their children attend; this appreciation, in turn, has led to special legal efforts that resulted in the Supreme Court decision on desegregation of the schools and in further implementation of that decision through the Civil Rights Act of 1964.

The nation at large is finding the road to school desegregation a long and tortuous path. Nevertheless, we seem to be moving ahead. An inch at a time, we are gradually moving in our public elementary and secondary schools toward the goal of quality education for every youngster, regardless of the color of his skin or the condition of his life.

In the meantime, it seems to me that we must speak more candidly than we have in the past of educational quality in our predominantly Negro colleges. We must face up to some hard questions about standards, and we must grope for some ingenious answers.

As a result of an extensive survey financed by the U.S. Office of Education at the request of Congress and made public three months ago, we now have more information about the inequities of segregated education than we ever had before. Regarding predominantly Negro colleges, the survey produced one finding which was, to me at least, a surprise. It showed that Negro colleges in general have a better ratio of students-to-faculty than other colleges.

But the survey also confirmed some disadvantages of Negro colleges that came as no surprise to anyone. Negro colleges have proportionately fewer Ph.D.'s on their faculties and pay them less than do other institutions. Further, because Negro colleges receive most of their students from segregated, inferior public schools, they must devote a substantial portion of their instructional time to remedial work. In consequence, the student who spends four years in a predominantly Negro institution may really have had only two or three years of college-level work.

Most Negro and white educators recognize these deficiencies in predominantly Negro institutions, and they appreciate the historical and economic reasons for them. But a kind of professional sympathy has prevented us from discussing as frankly as we should the necessary strategy for Negro institutions.

First, it seems to me that the predominantly Negro institutions cannot abandon the remedial function they have performed so well—a function which will continue to be an educational necessity for some years to come. Second, I would suggest that rather than rapidly expanding the range of courses they offer, most Negro colleges should concentrate their resources in the curricular areas they have already established, as long as these areas are pertinent to the world of employment and citizenship into which their graduates move. Third, more Negro institutions should raise their standards—not necessarily for admission, but certainly for graduation. As a practical matter, this might mean that some students in Negro colleges will spend five or six years in obtaining a bachelor's degree instead of the usual four. It will certainly mean that these institutions must give special attention to attracting and holding on their faculties persons of superior learning and competence. The investment required to attract top-level faculty is an economy in the long run; it will develop a different image of the whole institution, and it will move the level of learning on the campus more rapidly than any other single factor.

I realize that such suggestions run the risk of being offensive. I hope you will realize that they do not reflect on the ability of Negro students or the character of the institutions they attend. They do reflect the educational realities of segregated education during the twelve years before college. The Negro college, like other types of institutions, must shape its function around the educational backgrounds of the students it serves. And the students it serves, generally speaking, have been shortchanged by second-class, segregated education which must be dealt with, not merely deplored.

There is danger in generalizing about Negro or white institutions just as there is danger in generalizing about individuals. Hampton Institute offers a proud example of what can be achieved in terms of leadership and quality by dedicated efforts over the years. At the same time, I hope that its leaders are never satisfied and that they will be constantly seeking ways to improve quality and serve students more effectively.

As a further move to strengthen our Negro colleges, our best predominantly white institutions—both public and private —must do much more than they have in the past to lend some of their strength to the Negro colleges. Through passage of Title III of the Higher Education Act of 1965, the federal government has encouraged cooperative ventures between institutions that are on the way up and those that have already arrived. This program makes funds available to develop alliances with established universities for the improvement of quality in developing institutions. It is not, of course, restricted to predominantly Negro colleges, but they will be among its major beneficiaries. As institutions of higher education join together to serve our national purposes more effectively, they are reflecting the spirit which I believe must be fundamental to the Negro American's attitude toward our total society. He must seek to join with it and not to separate himself from it.

For better or for worse, like it or not, Negro American and white American are bound by a common hope and a common danger. We share a large piece of real estate, and it is this piece— not England, not Ireland, not Poland or Africa—which is our home. This land belongs to us, and if dissention rips it we will all share a common loss of a precious heritage.

Your special assignment is to use your wit and your wisdom to break the manacles that fetter the Negro to an inferior status in American life. But recognize that as Americans you wear invisible links that connect you with the American past and chain you to the American future. That future will bring you a generous measure of disappointment, a generous measure of occasions when it will seem more important to fight your way than to learn your way. But you must depend on learning, not only for the sake of the American Negro but also for the sake of the American white whose destiny as a free man is linked to yours.

Negro American and white American march together. We have not done too well in the past, perhaps, but we have begun to catch the cadence in recent years. And despite our regular failures, our regular missteps, we must keep moving forward together. The old phrase of the American Revolution has a new but important meaning for us in these times: "United we stand, divided we fall."

# CHAPTER 14

# EDUCATION—THE QUIET REVOLUTION

F OR IF we do not carefully and intelligently shape our present, time and
circumstance will dictate our future. And
every great nation that has in the past
abandoned struggle to rely on luck has
invariably discovered how fickle the lady
is.

From an address before the Annual Convention of the New York State School
Boards Association, Syracuse, New York, October 23, 1966.

# EDUCATION—THE QUIET REVOLUTION

NEXT YEAR, THE U. S. OFFICE OF EDUCATION WILL celebrate its 100th anniversary. Even though the event will probably not engender festivity in our corridors or commotion in the daily press, I find that this first century of OE operation offers a historical perspective that can be sustaining at times. The first Commissioner of Education had a staff of three and a salary of $4,000. The staff is 800 times larger today, and I wish that the salary were, too. In those moments when I question whether the rewards of government service outweigh the criticisms directed at the U. S. Office of Education, I find it helpful to recall that a Rhode Island farmer once threatened to shoot the first Commissioner of Education because of the radical proposals he advanced.

I would like to expand slightly on this historical perspective and consider not just the history of the U. S. Office of Education but that of the American public school system. The first Commissioner of Education, Henry Barnard, offers a focal point for the particular aspect of that history which I wish to discuss. The particular radical proposal to which the Rhode Island farmer objected, a proposal that Barnard advanced before becoming Commissioner, was this: He felt it would be a good idea if every American child could receive a free education in schools financed at the public expense.

A number of proposals advanced by the federal government and by the U. S. Office of Education in our day have been denounced as radical, as dangerous departures from American tradition. It seems to me worthwhile in evaluating these criticisms to consider what our tradition in education really is, to consider whether such "radical" proposals as federal aid to education, school desegregation, and the National Teacher Corps really depart from that tradition or whether, on the contrary, they extend it. My own contention is that rather than trying to go too far, too fast—as some critics allege—we have gone neither far enough nor fast enough. The evidence lies in the numbers of children in whom our schools seem unable to instill any love of learning or even any success in beginning it.

The American public school system came into being during the Jacksonian period of our history, roughly 1824 to 1850. The era brought with it a number of social, economic, and political reforms. This was, for example, the period when Dorothea Dix argued that the insane should be treated as patients, not caged like animals, and when an Illinois lawyer named Lincoln argued that slavery was morally wrong.

The reforms that eventually proved the weight of these arguments represented a triumph of humanitarian ideas, and there is no question that humanitarianism hastened the establishment of public schools. Yet several distinguished historians of education—Merle Curti, Sidney L. Jackson, and Paul Monroe among them—have demonstrated that the major arguments advanced for free education were not idealistic in nature. On the contrary, they were quite pragmatic. The proponents of free public schools did not say that this was the decent thing to do, or the charitable thing to do; they said it was the only *practical* thing to do. They argued that the American democracy in the first half of the nineteenth century was in danger of running riot and that free education was necessary to stabilize it, to prevent it from being destroyed by two contemporary developments in American life.

These developments were the widening of political suffrage and the rise of industry. By 1828, not only could most men in most states vote; more to the point, they actually did so. They could register at the ballot box their dissatisfactions with their lot. And the rise of industry during the first half of the nineteenth century made many Americans feel they had plenty to be dissatisfied about. Conditions of employment in the factories, mills, and mines were in many cases depressing and dangerous. Critics observed that lack of restraint among many of the new industrialists resulted in enormous profits for those on top of the system and a barely human level of subsistence for those on the bottom.

Reform was called for on every side, and the extension of the franchise made reform certain. But it was clear that if the ballot was to be an instrument for orderly change, the voters would have to exercise their franchise intelligently. While perceiving the necessity for change, they must appreciate also the necessity of being able to distinguish between promising solutions and the destructive nostrums of demagogues. They must, in short, be educated.

Thus, free public schools, although considered a radical institution in the first decades of the nineteenth century, were directed toward a basically conservative end. Rather than upsetting the established social order, they were designed to improve it. They were intended to harness new energies and desires to the proven worth of old institutions for the orderly growth of a nation which, having established its independence, had now to validate its maturity.

Our public schools helped achieve this end. By 1850, the principle of state-supported and state-supervised schools for all children had triumphed in the North and West. Free public schooling promised to offer the mass of Americans hope for the future when the present seemed to warrant little or none.

This promise was realized after the Civil War, when the great waves of immigration from Europe broke upon our shores. Had it not been for our public schools, the advent of millions of newcomers ignorant of our language and customs might have fragmented our single nation into a dozen competing enclaves. Once again, this so-called radical institution, free education, achieved a conservative end by stabilizing our democracy in the midst of forces that could have capsized it.

It seems to me that the United States today is contending with forces which, potentially at least, are as divisive and destructive as those which have threatened our nation in earlier years. Our new technology, while holding out to us the promise of a time when the most menial and unfulfilling tasks will be performed by machine, threatens also to create a new class of paupers whose unskilled labor continues to lose its value. The American Negro, quite suddenly militant after 100 years of comparative docility, demands freedom now from economic and social servitude and from second-class citizenship. Our cities, for decades ignored by rural-dominated legislatures, threaten to become factory towns ringed by surburban gardens that try to fence in city problems along with the city poor.

But we have finally recognized that we cannot fence those problems in. Despite our attempts to screen them from our view or otherwise ignore them, they force themselves upon our attention. The welfare rolls, the draft rejection rates, the hard-core unemployment that continues despite an unparalleled demand for skilled manpower touch every one of us no matter where we live, no matter what our economic or social condition. Crime, delinquency, unemployment, and the occasional violence stemming from the confused and inarticulate resentment of the poor do not observe the boundary lines on our maps. Once again we are forced to decide whether social reform and a better society will be shaped by intelligent voting and responsible local leadership, or by the emotional choices of frightened and angry men reacting to each other's fears and frustrations.

And once again, as we did during the Jacksonian period, we are experimenting with programs that perhaps, for some people, seem to smack of radicalism. After decades of opposition to federal aid for education, the American people reversed their position and produced a consensus on which the 88th and 89th Congresses acted with speed and force. The Elementary and Secondary Education Act of 1965 has already poured a billion dollars into our schools, and it has recently been extended to provide more aid. Federal loans and grants have been authorized to help insure that no capable youngster will be denied a higher education because he lacks the funds. Other federal programs for colleges and universities are making sure that there will be classroom space for our students. We have mounted a War on Poverty, an assault no other nation has seriously attempted. We are trying through the Job Corps to salvage young promise that has been blighted by poor family or educational background. Through such programs as the Volunteers in Service to America and the National Teacher Corps we are enlisting youthful energy and idealism in the national service. By means of such programs as Medicare, and through the creation of new governmental units such as Housing and Urban Development and the Department of Transportation, we are trying to develop solutions to the ages-old problems of the elderly and to the newer difficulties brought on by our conversion to a highly mobile, urban people. And finally, through the Civil Rights Act of 1964 and the establishment of legal principles by the federal courts, we are slowly eliminating the racial discrimination that has plagued one group of immigrants who came here long before the 13 colonies joined to form a nation.

Nor is the federal government the only source of imaginative new approaches to these problems. New York offers a number of examples of local and state programs that might serve as models to other states and communities throughout the country.

West Irondequoit and Rochester, for example, are cooperating in a program that brings Negro children from schools of the inner city to classes in a white suburb. I might add that the initiative for this program came from the white parents. Schools in Erie County and in Rockland County are pooling their resources to give children in these predominantly rural areas a wider variety of educational services than any school could offer individually— counseling, training for the handicapped, vocational education. More than 100 New York school districts are providing special educational and recreational services for the elderly. The State Department of Education, working with cultural institutions in

New York City, has exposed a million and a half children to the best in the fine and performing arts by busing them in from outlying communities. And I understand that your Department of Correction is experimenting with juvenile offenders to see if special educational programs can reduce the incidence of second offenses.

There is no question that these federal, state, and local activities taken together make up a program for progress unmatched in our history. We are embarked on a domestic revolution, a revolution financed by the majority to bring hope and opportunity to the minority.

Yet for all its "radicalism," this revolution—like that of the age of Jackson—has conservative ends. It is designed to preserve and strengthen, not to uproot and destroy. It is aimed not at overthrowing a social order that most of us have found to our liking but at admitting into that social order those millions whom racial injustice, the shortcomings of our schools, and the rapid development of our economy have excluded from the affluent society. We preserve our own freedoms most effectively by extending them to others. That concept is not what some have been pleased to term bleeding-heart liberalism; it is, rather, the hardest sort of pragmatism, and that is what this revolution is all about. Although it includes justice and fairness, this modern revolution is based also on practicality.

We have just begun this revolution. The enormous amounts of money that Congress has voted for aid to education have been invested so recently that it is not yet possible to gauge their effect accurately.

But it is clear that federal programs already have had a marked influence on the conduct of American education. Apart from the new buildings, the distribution of books to children, the construction of libraries where there never were libraries before, we can see a new spirit working in our schools and colleges. Teachers, principals, and professors—long aware of the deficiencies in our educational system, but up until recently powerless to do anything about them—are putting to work the ideas they have long advocated. Further, we are now drawing into this effort to improve American education the best minds of the business community.

Yet even as we begin to see promise in our programs to bring our worst schools up to the level of our best, it appears that the American people are approaching a crisis of confidence that could handicap the good work we have so recently begun. The riots of this summer have wakened in many white Americans a resentment of the measures they had previously approved to extend to children of the poor—many of whom are Negro Americans—a fuller and more just participation in our national life. It is this second matter that particularly concerns me, for such a resentment can hurt all our schools and all the children they serve, at the precise moment when we have begun to repair the neglect of decades.

The recent action of Congress in renewing the Elementary and Secondary Education Act of 1965 for two more years assures that supplemental funds will continue to flow to the poverty schools. But even \$2 billion or \$4 billion divided among all such schools in the nation works out to a comparatively small share for each. Federal spending and federal effort for education, no matter how much they may be increased in years to come, must be matched by increased support at the local and state levels. And it is at the local and state levels that the reaction to the new issues we confront can most severely hurt urban and rural slum schools.

As members of local school boards, I suspect you will encounter some of this reaction as you try to interpret educational needs to the citizens of your communities. I hope you will continue to argue for more financial support for our schools, even though you may be faced by demands for cutbacks.

I say this not in a partisan spirit, urging a Democratic program in place of a Republican, or a liberal program in preference to a conservative. I say it in the conviction that we must carry forward the broad program of social reform initiated in the past few years. We must do so, not only for the poor of our society but also for the privileged as well. A comfortable majority living alongside a deprived minority—whether poor white or poor black—is not really free to enjoy the fruits of its hard labors or good luck. It must live in constant expectation of such expressions of frustration and resentment as we witnessed these past two summers in Watts and Chicago and Atlanta. If we wish to preserve our own freedom to live in tranquility and in the rightful enjoyment of the American plenty, we must extend to others an equal opportunity to win a share of that plenty for themselves.

Education is the key to that opportunity. We know that American educational opportunity today is not equal for all citizens, and we have set about closing the gap between our best schools and our worst. If we succeed, we will not raise or reduce all members of our society to some mediocre common denominator, but we will give every one of them the chance to choose his own level of action and being, rather than forcing him to accept a life that circumstance has imposed. And if we fail, we will perpetuate within American democracy the divisions of race and of economic circumstance that now threaten our hard-won unity.

We have gone neither too fast nor too far in our revolution at home. Despite the setbacks, the second thoughts, and the occasional fatigue of spirit that inevitably accompany rapid change, we must proceed steadily. For if we do not carefully and intelligently shape our present, time and circumstance will dictate our future. And every great nation that has in the past abandoned struggle to rely on luck has invariably discovered how fickle the lady is.

Our history has been one of quiet but constant revolution. We must continue this tradition, recognizing that conservative ends sometimes require radical means. We are not the first Americans to have to choose between insuring the future by grasping the problems of the present or surrendering that future to our fears.

# MY GENERATION'S FINEST
# ACHIEVEMENT

Y OUR GENERATION is the one that made
the Peace Corps go, that by starting
the sit-ins at segregated lunch counters
started Negro Americans on a march that
will not be halted, that has questioned
the adult conduct of war abroad and of
peace at home—and made its influence
felt.

From an address before the Annual Westchester County Scholastic Achievement Dinner, Rye, New York, March 9, 1967.

# MY GENERATION'S FINEST
# ACHIEVEMENT

To A CASUAL OBSERVER, THIS MIGHT SEEM JUST ANother Thursday night. Actually, this is one of the most important Thursday nights in your lives. It marks your initiation into one of the magical practices and potent rituals of American adulthood—the after-dinner speech. If you had not distinguished yourselves in your studies, you could be home watching Batman, F Troop, Love on a Rooftop, the Dean Martin Show, and Perry Mason. Instead you are going to listen to the U.S. Commissioner of Education.

I want you all to sit still and take it like soldiers. Afterdinner speeches build character. And if any of you fidgets or whispers to your neighbor, I will turn you in to the CIA and you will lose your subsidy.

After-dinner speeches build character, that is, for everyone except the speaker. Preparing a talk for teenagers seems to bring out the worst in many adults. Despite the fact that every one of us spent seven long and arduous years as teenagers, most of us find it difficult to decide what to talk to you about. If I were addressing colleagues in education or government, I could come up with half a dozen topics without pausing to think twice.

I could, for example, discuss the pros and cons of team teaching, weigh the relationships between a school board and its superintendent, or analyze the federal-state-local partnership. I even have a couple of humorous anecdotes to go with each, and people who work for me assure me they are very funny stories, no matter what anyone else says.

But unfortunately for me, few sensible teenagers give a hang about team teaching or the federal role in education. From what I have observed, teenagers wonder about things like life, death, love, and happiness. They mix their curiosity about these topics with questions about others which parents tend to dismiss as trivial—such as, can I have the car Friday night, and how come it's all right for *you* to use words like that when you get mad but not me? In general, however, teenagers appear to want to get a handle on the big questions. They want to know about The World. And recognizing this, adult speakers tend to take one of two tacks.

First, they give advice. They warn the supposedly naive young of the pitfalls that await them, hold up for their admiration various examples of adult rectitude and valor, and enjoin the young audience to go and do likewise.

Or, on the other hand, they confess with bogus candor that their own generation has made a botch of things and express the hope that your generation will take over the administration of the world without delay. This approach might be called the passing-on-the-flag ploy; its effectiveness is vastly increased if the speaker delivers his remarks in a faltering voice and stumbles at the podium to symbolize the essential senility of his generation.

Attractive as these alternate courses are, I intend to avoid both of them tonight. For the first ignores the fact that teenagers have been receiving advice all their lives and that they have developed enough perception to suspect some of it and enough maturity to resent all of it. As for the second, I am not at all convinced that my generation has done such a bad job with the world. Nor do I believe yours is going to do a lot better. In any case, I suspect that most elderly people—those over 30—are not yet ready to declare themselves out of the game. Tattered and drooping as the banner of mankind may be, most of us still want to help wave the flag for a little while longer.

So I do not intend to give advice tonight nor to ask you to take over the world quickly, before we ancients fumble it away. But I would like to talk about the state of that world, to develop a sort of world-view. I launch into this undertaking not with the idea of asking you to accept my appraisal of our society's assets and liabilities but with the feeling that it might offer you a basis of comparison for developing your own. Unpleasant as the prospect undoubtedly seems to many members of my generation, the fact is that the members of yours *are* on the way toward running our world—and if you're going to do a decent job of it, you will need some sort of general viewpoint about this globe which is our home.

I'd like to begin by going back to something I said earlier: that I am not at all convinced, despite some evidence to the contrary, that my generation has done such a bad job of conducting the second and third quarters of the twentieth century. Every generation tries to anticipate what's going to happen in its lifetime and to plan for the needs it discerns. But every generation must, in addition, deal with the accidents of history—with those global happenings that exceed the power of any human to predict.

Perhaps the most important accidents my generation dealt with were World War II and the atomic bomb. Both those events altered our world in ways which we have yet to appreciate fully. The simplest way to characterize that alteration may be to say that the events of the 1940's swung the pendulum of human belief to the other end of its arc.

The nineteenth century, by and large, was a period of optimism, an era of sunny expectation which continued into the first part of the twentieth. The Industrial Revolution, with its increased productivity for every worker, appeared to offer man the vision of a new world of abundance for all. The nationalistic movements in Europe created a certain amount of political conflict as tiny duchies and medieval states merged to form larger units; even so, the citizens of emergent nations such as Germany and Italy saw in their new unity an end to the bickering which had sapped their resources and prevented them from achieving identity and dignity as a people. Darwin's theory of biological evolution helped inspire a host of new theories of moral evolution: if the human organism had by adaptation gained dominance over the rest of the physical world, perhaps the human spirit was evolving, too, constantly drawing closer to a state of angelic perfection. This was, in the main, a period of belief in human perfectibility, typified in the slogan preached by the French psychotherapist Émile Coué: "Every day and in every way, I am becoming better and better."

Not even World War I fully stifled this spirit of optimism. In those days, it was the "Great War," not World War I, for we didn't anticipate having to add a II. The Great War was the "war to preserve democracy," the "war to end all wars." Certainly that was something to be optimistic about, even if thousands of people did get killed in the quest for peace.

But after the war this optimism ebbed, as we struggled with the question of military armament to keep the peace, as economic depression swept Europe and the United States, as a former corporal named Adolph Hitler, building on the resentment and confusion of his defeated people, announced a new crusade based on a gospel of racial superiority. And after we had defeated Hitler, people around the globe found it difficult to decide which was worse: the human depravity unveiled in the German concentration camps or the technological horror revealed in the bombings of Hiroshima and Nagasaki. Man, the prince of creation, seemed to have turned his back on the stars, to have created a new jungle which promised devastation for all and survival for none.

We have been living with the prospect of self-annihilation for 20 years now, and every one of those years has added its own quotient of trouble to our other burdens. Overseas, we have tried to contend with the growth of communism, and with nationalistic developments in Africa, Asia, and Latin America which threatened or seemed to threaten our own welfare. At home, although more people have more money, more leisure, more education, and more hope for the future than at any time in our past, we have been challenged by new enemies: air pollution, the decline of our cities, the contamination of our water, the human erosion of our natural resources. And we have finally awakened to problems created by ancient enemies: poverty and racial discrimination.

We have, in short, much to be pessimistic about. The adult who wants to use the passing-on-the-flag ploy has many defeats to document the failure of his generation.

Yet it seems to me that the pendulum of belief, having swung from optimism to darkest pessimism, is headed back now in the other direction. We may never recapture the optimism your grandparents' generation felt early in this century—and that will be all to the good, for much of that optimism ignored the squalid underside of industrial progress. But my generation has seen some hope breaking through the spiritual blackout of the 1940's, and that hope must be included in any reckoning of my generation's balance sheet.

We have known for more than 20 years now how to blow up the world. And although there's no guarantee that it won't happen before you enter college next fall, it hasn't happened yet. For years now, we have been engaging in negotiations with the Soviet Union to ward off the possibility that one of us will obliterate the other. A sizeable sector of American political comment views these negotiations as useless; I don't, and I have lots of respectable company. It seems possible that, along with developing the means for unlimited destruction, man can also develop the discipline to restrain himself in the use of unlimited power. This is a cautious hope, but we have no real choice except to explore it. If we do not somehow manage to live together, we shall, quite simply, die together.

It seems to me that the years since 1960 have afforded us other reasons for cautious hope in international political developments. Human freedom, repressed as it is in large sections of the globe, nevertheless seems to be on the march in surprising places. Writers in Soviet Russia, Poland, and other countries of eastern Europe are saying nasty things about their governments —and getting away with it. What is still referred to by many columnists as the "Communist bloc" seems to be disintegrating, and it appears that not even the thought of Mao will be mighty enough to stick it back together again. Red China, in fact—the most militant exponent of hard-line communism—looks as if it is going to provide our times with an object lesson in how *not* to run a revolution.

Such slight but undeniable alterations in the political climate overseas have been matched by genuine changes here at home, too. Above all, I would say that since World War II we have gained an ability to recognize our own deficiencies, to realize that Americans are as fallible as any other group of human beings and, because of our wealth, power, and influence, have correspondingly more chances to make international fools of ourselves. We have recognized the fact that empty stomachs usually have different politics than full ones; so instead of sending fleets around the world to demonstrate our power, we are sending seeds and tractors, technicians and generators around the world to demonstrate our new prudence.

At home we have begun in a faltering way to be honest with ourselves about our treatment of racial minorities. Our courts, our Congress, and our national conscience—for the first time in 100 years of post-Civil War history—are acting together to seek for Negro Americans the rights we have long denied them.

Such manifestations of national maturity both at home and abroad strike me as causes for hope, for a belief that a middle-aged generation which spent its youth in war can fashion for its inheritors a reasonably promising time in which to begin adulthood. This is, if you like, a personal return to optimism which might seem to disregard all the national and international causes for despair.

But despair seems to me unwarranted, largely and finally because of what I regard as the finest achievement of my generation: your generation. I do not intend to wind up these remarks with a mindless paean to American youth, for genetically I don't believe you offer any finer examples of human nature than my generation did.

Nevertheless, it seems to me there has been a qualitative change in young American men and women. Your generation is the one that made the Peace Corps go, that by starting the sit-ins at segregated lunch counters started Negro Americans on a march that will not be halted, that has questioned the adult conduct of war abroad and of peace at home—and made its influence felt.

This kind of student concern marks a dramatic change since my college days. Undergraduates of my generation rarely interested themselves in anything that took place off the campus. From their point of view, colleges and universities were tight little islands, separated from the mainland of human activity by four years of disengagement.

The young men and women a few years ahead of you have changed all that, and they have raised adult tempers in the process—sometimes for good reason, sometimes not. But the net result of all this student activity has been to force adults to pay attention to some concerns which we either had not noticed or had written off as hopeless causes. I believe we adults are better off for the slings and arrows which your outraged generation has hurled at us, and that your children's world will be a better one because our children rejected apathy.

A young man named Jack Newfield has written a fine book about the most vocal members of your vocal generation. It's called *The Prophetic Minority*. In the main, it discusses the various groups of the New Left—the radical movement which draws its origins and support from our colleges. Mr. Newfield closes his book with two paragraphs that I would like to quote in full:

The New Radicals are speaking harsh truths in a new and irreverent voice. They are saying that communism is changing, and that positions frozen a decade ago must be reconsidered. They are saying that the whole society—from the academy to the anti-poverty program—has become too bureaucratized and must be decentralized and humanized. They are saying the draft is undemocratic. They are saying that revolutions are tearing the colonial clamps off three continents, and that America must stand with the poor and not the powerful. They are saying that automation is making a guaranteed annual income and a redefinition of work imperative. They are say-

ing that ethics and politics have become divided and must be re-
united.

If they are emotional or badly informed about other things, on all
these issues the New Radicals are right. The older dissenters should
pause and acknowledge these new voices before the Generation Gap
becomes a canyon of mistrust.

I do not share Mr. Newfield's conviction that the New Radicals are right about *all* these issues; that is irrelevant to the
purpose of my remarks tonight. But I am concerned with the
possibility that the gap between our generations—a difference
not only of years, but also of points of view born at different
times—will become a "canyon of mistrust," a separation that
prevents us from talking to each other.

It is most important that we continue to talk to each other,
not only as parents and children, but as equals in a society which
can benefit from my generation's experience as well as from your
generation's dissent. Moreover, the burden of maintaining that
conversation does not fall entirely on the older members of our
society. The younger dissenters should pause and acknowledge
that if their mothers and fathers have been blind in many ways,
if they have failed in many endeavors, they have nevertheless
created a society in which young people can stand up to their
elders, look them straight in the eye, and tell them they're
wrong.

We're not always wrong. Your generation suggests to me that
mine has reared a crop of free men and women, and that when
it is time for you to take over our national flag, you will wave it
as highly and proudly as any of us could wish.

Until then, try to talk to Mom and Dad. They need sympathy,
for—like most parents—they had children. And that's one problem I don't think even *your* generation will solve.

# CHAPTER 16

# IN DEFENSE OF USELESSNESS

I HOPE that you will continue to pay equal attention to the "useful" and the "useless" sides of higher learning, for a society in which everyone could program a computer but no one could wonder at a snowflake would be dreary indeed.

---

From an address given at the dedication of the Fine and Applied Arts Building, Fairmont State College, Fairmont, West Virginia, March 19, 1967.

# IN DEFENSE OF USELESSNESS

OST ORGANIZATIONS TAKE THEMSELVES SERI-
ously most of the time; during centennial years, they tend
to regard themselves with awe. Since both Fairmont State
College and the U. S. Office of Education are celebrating
their 100th anniversaries this year, we both run the risk of
collapsing under self-esteem during 1967.

Perhaps we can be forgiven for succumbing to a degree of pride this year. Both of us have come a long way.

Fairmont started out in the basement of a church, with
a student body of 30 and a faculty of 2. The U. S. Office
of Education might be said to have started out in the
basement of federal government. It was established with
the lukewarm support of most Congressmen and over the
flat opposition of a few. After one year of operation, its
staff of four was reduced to three, and the Commissioner's
salary of $4,000 was cut by 25 percent.

Today, Fairmont has a faculty, staff, and student body
of about 2,600, and the U. S. Office of Education has approximately that number of personnel. Judging from your
campus and the size of our Congressional appropriations,
I would say that both of us have climbed the stairs from
the basement of our respective jurisdictions to the lobby
floor.

Yet neither buildings nor dollars offer an adequate
index to the character of an institution. Nor does age:
100 years can bring wisdom and experience, but they can

also bring senility. No organization exists for its own sake. There is only one adequate measure of the success of any assemblage of people and buildings: the degree to which it carries out the purpose for which it was established.

This purpose can be determined with relative ease for most enterprises. The purpose of a business concern is to make money in a legitimate way, and if it fails in that, it fails completely—regardless of how many fine things it does in the name of public relations or corporate citizenship. The purpose of a hospital is to cure illness; of a government agency, to perform the tasks assigned it by Congress and the Administration; and of an orchestra, to make music.

Similarly, the purpose of an educational institution would seem to be easy to define: It is to educate.

Yet that simple formulation has probably inspired more prose than any other human concerns except love and war. Four thousand years after Plato tried his hand at defining what a good education is, we are still attempting to figure the matter out for ourselves. We all agree these days that every American child should have what we term a "quality education," and we have set about trying to remedy those social and financial circumstances that have prevented many American youngsters from receiving it in the past. But we still do not agree precisely on what a quality education is, how it is brought about, and what effects it should produce in its possessors.

Debates about these questions are lively enough in grammar and high school circles. The debates are even louder among college and university educators, for as subject matter becomes more diverse and complex, it opens correspondingly larger areas for disagreement. And much of the disagreement today centers around one question: What *is* a higher education?

Many people tend to think of higher education as a vocational sort of process—a period of study which qualifies a youngster for a better job, a time for acquiring the skills and knowledge other people will pay for. And clearly, a person is likely to make more money by going to college than he would by ending his education with a high school diploma.

This view is borne out by figures. We know that, on the average, a man with an eighth-grade education can expect to earn $180,000 over the course of his lifetime; if he goes on to earn a high school diploma, he will make about $246,000; and if he obtains a college degree, he can expect a lifetime income of $386,000.

So there is plain bread-and-butter wisdom behind this conviction that a young man or woman who invests four years of tuition and effort in a college education ought to be able to turn those years to financial account. Beyond that, there is an important social wisdom in this vocational emphasis. We live in a technological age which places a premium on scientific achievement and on the application of principles discovered in the laboratory to everyday life. Our position in the family of nations requires us to maintain our scientific and technological leadership, and that in turn demands large numbers of highly trained recruits for our research laboratories and for business and industry. Finally, the pace of technological change has made and will continue to make many skills and jobs obsolete; an individual's survival as an economic unit, as a person capable of providing for himself and his family, depends on his developing a sufficiently high order of expertise in some field to guarantee him continued employment.

All these statements are fairly obvious, and they have been repeated at tiresome length in many other places. In fact, I have the uneasy feeling that I am stating them at tiresome length today. I echo them here for two reasons: first, to point up the contrast between the amount of attention we pay to the "useful" side of higher education as against the "useless" side; second, to advance the thesis that the "useless" part of higher education —useless in the sense of having no immediate, clearly practical application—may well be the more important.

The building we are dedicating today—a building which will serve the fine arts and the applied arts alike—symbolizes both in name and in function these two aspects of higher education and the tension between them. The applied arts are useful arts; they result in a tangible product—a thumb tack or a suspension bridge—which confers some measurable benefit on the user. By contrast, the fine arts provide most of us with no immediately useful product for daily living; only in rare cases is there sufficient commercial carry-over from the study of painting or music to enable the student to earn a living from these difficult disciplines. The fine arts—and, by extension, many of the courses which our college curricula lump under the heading of "humanities"—are utterly useless by any usual meaning of that word.

Why, then, do we spend any time on them at all? Largely, I believe, because of the important distinction between *use* and *value*. The vocational aspect of higher education is important and not to be disparaged. Yet anyone who has observed his college and high school classmates make their way through the world for two decades or so realizes how few of them wind up doing today what they intended 20 years ago. This means that vocational choices made in the early 1920's are often suspect, and that at least part of a higher education must be designed to give a student the intellectual flexibility to shift his course and develop new plans after he has embarked on a career. I would suggest that the study of the humanities, with which I include the arts, can help to build this flexibility.

Yet the basic value of the humanities in higher education curricula does not depend on any indirect utility they may have for a job. Their basic value resides not in what the student can do *with* them, but what they do *for* him, as a person living with himself.

Every one of us spends his life as a member of various societies, ranging in size from the family to the nation. We are fathers or mothers, sisters or brothers, sons or daughters. In addition, we are citizens of a community and of a state, and each of these relationships imposes certain responsibilities on us—responsibilities that, in many instances, education fits us to discharge more intelligently.

One would expect, for example, that a man who has developed a lifelong habit of reading would be able to vote more perceptively than a man who reads nothing. One would expect that a man who has been trained to view his world through some sort of historical perspective would be able to appreciate the possible consequences that problems today will have on his community or family several years from now.

Such instances point to the social value of those aspects of higher education which cannot be immediately or directly converted into personal gain through a job. And yet, beyond even this social value of education, there is a personal value which may ultimately be the most important single result of higher education. Although we spend most of our time with other human beings—with co-workers, friends, members of our family—there are many hours when each of us is alone. It is at such moments that we best appreciate the fact that underlying our various roles as citizens, parents, and wage-earners, there resides a unique personality which cannot be adequately defined in terms of functions. This personality, a puzzling legacy of heredity and environment and something else which gives each of us a distinctive way of looking at things and feeling about things, can only be described as our *self*.

This self has its needs, too, and they cannot be met wholly by shelter, food, or companionship. Primarily they are needs of the spirit and the soul, but they are just as real as the craving for sustenance or the instinct for survival. They are needs for meaning in life, for self-respect, for a sense of participation in the unique capacity of the human being to rise above animal existence and create a civilization.

It is this appetite, this dimly understood need, which the humanities, the fine arts, the "useless" side of higher education is intended to satisfy. Thus though the humanities may have absolutely no *use* in the ordinary meaning of that word, they have a profound *value*. *Hamlet* tells us virtually nothing about the past history of Denmark, nor does it offer us lessons in history or political science that can be applied to our own public affairs today. But *Hamlet* does remind us that other men in other times knew the profound loneliness of personal dilemmas, and it can help in hours of individual stress to know that isolation and fear, doubt and discouragement are continuing conditions of man. Poetry and music and art give us a continuing share in all of human nature, enabling us to step outside our own restricted lives to participate in the sometimes stumbling, sometimes ennobling efforts of man to understand himself and his position in the world he has inherited. The humanities constitute a great conversation across the ages by which Socrates can speak to us with as much freshness and pertinence as the television commentator on the 6:00 p.m. news broadcast.

It is quite possible that educators in the past have given too much weight to the humanities. Indeed, at one point in the development of English and American higher education, any study which could be converted to practical use was suspect for that reason.

The pendulum has swung to the practical side of the curriculum. The tendency these days is to stress the pragmatic aspects of higher education, the fact that a college degree can qualify a young man or woman for a higher paying job than he could otherwise obtain. Overemphasis on the practical in American education seems to me a matter of deep concern. In connection with our schools, we frequently hear music, the dance, and the fine arts described as "frills" to be dispensed with first in the face of a squeeze on the budget.

O. Henry wrote a short story about two prospectors who became snowbound for the winter in an Alaskan cabin. They had two books: *The Rubaiyat of Omar Khayyam* and the *World Almanac*. Each took one book and learned it by heart. When the snow melted, they returned to San Francisco and by chance fell in love with the same girl. In every crisis the man who knew the facts came to the rescue. But the man who grasped the spirit of "A Jug of Wine, a Loaf of Bread—and Thou/Beside me singing in the Wilderness . . ." got the girl. Perhaps the humanities are not so unimportant after all!

We will never develop a formula which will parcel out the

undergraduate's time in ideal proportions to the vocational and nonvocational aspects of the curriculum. As with so many human choices, this choice will always require some judgment, some experience, and a little bit of hunch, as well as an attempt to tailor the educational program to the needs of individual students.

The fact that Fairmont is today dedicating a building to be used for both the applied and fine arts shows that you are aware of the dual purpose of higher education and that you do not intend to slight the humanistic to favor the pragmatic. I hope that you will continue to pay equal attention to the "useful" and the "useless" sides of higher learning, for a society in which everyone could program a computer but no one could wonder at a snowflake would be dreary indeed.

# CHAPTER 17

# NATIONAL POLICY FOR
# AMERICAN EDUCATION

B UT THE fact remains that parents'
groups and other citizens' organizations do influence educational policy by
presenting various viewpoints on issues
in education. Although you may not
write policy as members of the PTA, you
do so as voters.

From an address before the 71st Annual Convention of the National Congress
of Parents and Teachers, Minneapolis, Minnesota, May 22, 1967.

# NATIONAL POLICY FOR AMERICAN EDUCATION

E DUCATION MAY BE THE ONLY SERVICE INDUSTRY which continues to flourish despite the fact that it forces the customer to take what he gets, like it or not. Most American youngsters have only one choice of school: the one nearest their homes. And even though private and parochial schools offer an alternative to the public school in many communities, attendance at these is as often based upon social or religious considerations as on any presumed academic superiority.

In recent years, college students have begun demanding a larger voice in shaping their education. Elementary and secondary students, however, remain a silent clientele. That is why parent groups, such as the PTA, are so important to American education. They provide a means by which the juvenile customer of the business—at least through his parental representatives—can cast a vote for or against management.

I realize that the PTA has a tradition of not interfering in matters of educational administration. That is a sound position, and I do not intend to suggest any modification of it. But the fact remains that parents' groups and other citizens' organizations do influence educational policy by presenting various viewpoints on issues in education. Although you may not write policy as members of the PTA, you do so as voters. What I would like to do today, therefore, is to invite your consideration of my viewpoint on some matters of educational policy that will undoubtedly affect our schools for generations to come.

One matter is the relationship of the federal to state and local governments in the direction and financing of education. As you probably know, the Constitution confers absolutely no educational responsibility on the federal government. It leaves education in the hands of the states, and the states, in turn, have delegated the responsibility for managing the schools to local communities.

How, then, did the federal government attain its present influence in educational affairs?

You have all heard the Sputnik and Selma explanations before, so I will not try your patience by rehearsing those lines again. By looking beneath those proper names and other specific events which inspired federal investment in schools and colleges, I think we can discern a common theme in Washington's involvement in educational affairs: a recognition that some educational problems are common to every part of our country, that they are of sufficient gravity to affect American citizens generally, and that state and local governments have not the resources to solve these problems.

In recent years, for example, the federal government has addressed itself to the difficulty that youngsters from low-income families experience in getting to college. This is a large problem for the nation because we need highly trained manpower in a hundred new occupations and most of the old ones. It is a problem for individuals because, in an industrially sophisticated society such as ours, the lack of a higher education disqualifies intellectually able men and women for the most fulfilling, interesting occupations. And although some states and many communities had gone to extraordinary lengths to offer scholarship assistance and tax-supported higher education, it was obvious that hundreds of thousands of youngsters who would benefit from college instruction could not hope to obtain it. We know, for example, that in 1960 the son of a family with an annual income of $12,000 had three times as much chance of entering college as the son of a family with a $3,000 annual income, even though both boys had precisely the same academic aptitude. Such considerations produced the variety of federal programs we have today to help able students get into college and stay there.

Another problem which the Congress judged sufficiently weighty to require federal attention was the education of culturally deprived children. It became clear that youngsters in our urban and rural slums were not receiving an education pertinent to their special needs. Such an education had to be of a different kind than most school districts offered. It had to take these children's backgrounds into account, to recognize that they entered school without the educational head start that an economically favored home provides. Such education, moreover, is very expensive; few school districts had the resources either to design such an education or to support it.

Operation Head Start and Title I of the Elementary and Secondary Education Act represent the federal response to this national problem. We don't believe for a moment that such programs represent final or even adequate solutions to the problem of educating the disadvantaged. But they do represent a recognition that this is a *national* problem, not peculiar to a single state or region, and they enable the states and localities to direct educational energies toward solving it.

Thus the federal thrust in education may be seen in two lights. First, it is intended to serve individuals and provide a new reach for quality in educating them. Second, it is directed at national concerns that relate intimately to the future strength of our society and its ability to survive in a large, contentious family of nations. And what this process of singling out national issues in education has resulted in is a system of categorical aids: programs intended to serve a specific purpose, rather than the broad purposes of education generally. If you take a hostile view of categorical aid, I suppose you can say that it amounts to this sort of position: The federal government tells the states and localities they must perform this or that particular educational task if they want money from Washington. This categorical aid approach is in contrast to a general aid approach, which would give funds to the states for any educational purpose they choose.

Whatever its limitations, the categorical aid approach gives the states and local communities a great deal of leeway in designing educational programs to meet various needs. In essence, the federal government says to the states: "Here is some money to solve this particular problem; you figure out how to do it."

Today the categorical approach is being attacked as representing an unwarranted intrusion of the federal government into state and local educational affairs. There is a great deal of interest today on the part of state and local governments in general aid to education. Partially, I suspect, this stems from the human dislike for having someone else—in this case, the Congress of the United States—tell you what to do, even indirectly. Partially it stems from an irritation over the red tape that federal programs involve for states and local school systems. This criticism is justified, to a degree, and the U. S. Office of Education has been taking steps to reduce the administrative detail involved in obtaining federal funds.

But whatever the criticisms which can in justice be leveled against categorical aid to education, I believe that we must stick with it, rather than electing general aid as an alternative. The postwar period has radically altered the demands we place on our schools; a purely local or state viewpoint of education cannot produce an educational system that will serve national interests in addition to more localized concerns.

This viewpoint, called *localism*, has in the past been the keynote of American education. It regarded the school's main task as that of training a youngster to live as an adult in the community of his birth. Although American schools have a common allegiance to some basic educational principles, each of them also reflects the distinctive economic, social, historical, and intellectual realities of its community.

Today we must question the validity of excessive localism in education. I am not questioning the American tradition of vesting control of the schools with the local taxpayers, nor suggesting that a national government should decide what is to be taught. I am saying that we must recognize the fact that changes are taking place within our society which make it likely that a boy educated in Mississippi or New York City will spend his adult life in New Mexico or Atlanta. This means that an education rooted in local circumstances may well be irrelevant to the environment in which a student spends his adult life. This means, further, that the national government—the one we all pay for— does have a legitimate interest in what the states and localities do in the name of education. Every person born in the United States is a citizen of this country. Certainly no one will argue that it is fair or reasonable to deny him equality of educational opportunity because he happens to have been born in a community that refuses to support good education.

Further, we should recognize that the categorical aid approach evolved from a long and stormy struggle over the question of whether the federal government should support education at all. In 1948, Senator Taft changed his earlier position and came out in support of federal aid to education. His words on that occasion are worth quoting:

"In matters affecting the necessities of life," he told the Senate, "I do not believe the federal government can . . . say to the people, 'Go your way and do the best you can.'

"Because of the way wealth is distributed in the United States," he continued, "I think we have the responsibility to see if we cannot eliminate hardship, poverty, and inequality of opportunity to the best of our ability. I do not believe we are able to do it without a federal aid system."

With Senator Taft's support, a bill for general aid to education passed the Senate. However, it did not get by the House. In fact, if it were not for the categorical approach to aid education, it is doubtful that we would have any federal aid to education today at all. For categorical aid represents a compromise among perfectly respectable but varying special interests. It represents a financial program on which a number of otherwise dissenting parties can agree. Whatever officials in public, parochial, and private school systems may think about their role in the future of American education, at least they have managed to ignore their differences when it comes to certain specific educational needs of children. Categorical aid, in short, represents a major triumph of the American political system.

Moreover, I believe that categorical aid should always be an integral feature of federal support of education. Perhaps in years to come it will no longer be necessary to concentrate on the special needs or categories to which we direct our national interest today—education of the disadvantaged, for instance, or education of the handicapped. But there will be other categories of national concern which will require our attention. Rather than rejecting out of hand the principle of categorical aid in favor of general aid, what we must do is find a proper blend of the two.

The U. S. Office of Education has no plans to submit to Congress a general aid program at this time. Nor can I say when we will. But looking toward the future, I believe that a general aid program will eventually come. It will come because state and local tax resources combined are still inadequate to support education of the quality Americans expect for their children.

When general aid does come, it must combine four elements.

First, a general aid program must have built into it a guarantee that local and state support of education will continue so that federal dollars do not merely replace other dollars and provide no additional benefits to children.

Second, it must have an equalization factor which takes into account each state's financial abilities and insures that the states which need more help receive more. Further, this equalization factor must prevent the states from short-changing their cities. Most states today are simply not doing what they should for urban education.

Third, general aid must provide a foundation of support— a financial floor of aid from federal sources—to every state. It must not become merely a device for taking money from the rich states and redistributing it to the poor ones. It must instead guarantee new educational opportunities for all our children.

Fourth, it must assume the continuation of large categorical aid programs so that important national problems can continue to receive attention after broad, basic support is introduced.

In connection with this matter of "important national problems," I would like to comment on improving educational opportunities for racial minorities. This issue is part and parcel of our national effort to serve better in the schools those children who come from disadvantaged homes and who bring to school with them an initial learning handicap. It is simply a fact of American life that a very high proportion of Negro, Puerto Rican, Mexican-American, and Indian children are the children of parents who cannot give them the advantages most Americans have come to expect for their children. It is no accident that an unreasonably large percentage of our poor come from our racial minorities. If we are honest with ourselves, we have to admit that the education, the employment, the living conditions, and the health services which public policy and private decision have made available to these citizens have been second rate. Where we have changed public policy to bring equal treatment, these minorities still suffer the stigma of private discrimination.

This nation is engaged in a great crusade aimed at giving all citizens equal opportunity to achieve their potential, irrespective of race, religion, or national origin. The schools are central to that crusade. The great Elementary and Secondary Education Act of 1965 contains the fundamental implication that it is our national purpose to use federal funds to help the schools do a better job for our educationally neglected children. I say "educationally neglected" because these are the children with whom the schools have failed. These children make up a major share of our 1,000,000 annual dropouts from school. Many of them start with failure in first grade and continue that frustrating experience until they leave school with inadequate skills and no job possibilities.

For the children of our urban and rural slums, the Elementary and Secondary Education Act holds a message of hope. It recognizes that to provide true equality of educational opportunity and to make up for the disadvantages of poverty, it is necessary to expend more effort and more money per child. They need smaller classes, remedial teachers, health services, better nutrition, modern classroom equipment, and a variety of other special additions to what they normally find in school. They need, also, specially trained teachers and extra effort to connect the school and the home in a common purpose of success in education.

But these children need something else as well. They need to believe that they have an equal chance with other Americans, regardless of differing racial and cultural characteristics. And they will never believe this as long as they are segregated, as long as they are not permitted to associate in school with the white majority. That memorable phrase of the Declaration of Independence, "We hold these truths to be self-evident, that all men are created equal . . .," will continue to have a hollow sound to these children as long as the white people who control opportunity find a way within or without the law to continue racial isolation for minorities in our public schools.

I mention these matters because of a serious policy problem I see confronting the schools of our country. It is the issue of a split between those who advocate programs like the Elementary and Secondary Education Act and those who reject such programs and seek racial integration as the sole solution to the problems of racially isolated groups of children.

On the one hand we find developing a viewpoint which says: "You can't integrate the children in our central cities. It isn't practical. There's no manageable plan which will work. Therefore, let's forget integration and make massive investments in improving the quality and services of the schools."

On the other hand there is a counterview which says: "The only way to success for the racially isolated child is to get rid of his racial isolation. Compensatory education through broader and better school services hasn't worked in the past and won't work now. Since white people control the schools and funds to operate them, the only way to get good schools for Negroes and other racial minorities is to integrate. Then the white people will care about what's going on in the schools and do something about it."

My concern is that we may develop these two views into two strongly opposing camps, each seeking to advance its policy in the schools. My firm belief is that both policies must be pursued at the same time. We must provide special services for the children of the poor to help them catch up. At the same time we must express in the public schools the beliefs professed in our public utterances, in our civil rights legislation, and in the decisions of our courts. We publicly pay lip service to the proposition that racial segregation is discriminatory. Yet we continue to organize our schools on a segregated basis and to support such arrangements with the rationalization that children should go to school in their neighborhood and that the schools can't be blamed for the fact that the neighborhood is either all white or all Negro.

Looking at this seemingly irrefutable combination of facts, the reasoning person sees that two types of change are possible to move toward a solution—change in who lives in a particular neighborhood on one hand; and, on the other, change in which children go to school with each other. Both of these changes are difficult to bring about. Neither can be made on a massive basis all at once. But dedicated school boards, city planners, and political leaders can start on both.

To my mind, one of the hopeful developments of the past five years has been the vigor of local school boards in addressing themselves to these problems. Even five years ago in most of our cities the problems of racial isolation were not on the school board agenda. Today, there is scarcely a city in the nation which isn't at least discussing the problem, and there are many which are doing something about it. Some cities have begun to establish new relationships with the surburbs around them and to exchange pupils for special purposes which benefit both suburb and city. Some are planning building programs which will bring better services to all pupils and at the same time bring new pupil associations across economic and racial lines.

Whatever the solution being tried, there is a kind of local initiative being exercised today which was not in the air a few short years ago. And it is local initiative which in the great majority of cases is not required by any state or federal law or by pressures from the U. S. Office of Education. No federal imperatives require a city without a dual school system to take action to diminish its *de facto* segregation. But many cities are doing so because their leaders are concerned about the limitation of opportunity imposed on Americans who are subjected to segregation.

The toughest problems are those of the great metropolitan centers. Experiments in integration in such medium-sized communities as Rochester, Hartford, Sacramento, Berkeley, and others just don't seem applicable to New York City or to the 90 percent Negro population in the schools of Washington, D. C. Perhaps these great centers of racial isolation will be the last to change. Maybe the problems must grow worse before we can develop the local resolution to do what is necessary to start the uphill struggle toward a better future. In the meantime, we must keep both objectives before us and continue to improve the quality of education for the children of the ghetto while we seek ways to bring them into contact with children who have had a different home experience. On this second front we must work just as hard to change the ghetto as we strive to help children to reach outside it.

Many of you PTA members are from communities where the problems of which I speak seem far away. Perhaps you have no racial minorities or, if you have them, they present no massive problems of isolation and deprivation. Many of you come from suburbs which have no contact with America's poor. To you, these issues may seem irrelevant. But to those involved in this insulation, I would make two observations:

1. You and your children have your share of responsibility as Americans for the conditions which leave a significant number of your fellow citizens without hope.

2. Your children will live in a more crowded and more complex world than the world of today. It will be a world in which our cities are either centers of culture and hope or centers of conflict and despair, depending on what you and I do today about them. We cannot solve all these problems through the schools, but we can make a start.

Putting together what I have said to you about categorical aid from the federal government, about general aid to our schools from the same source, and about the special needs of our poor and our racially isolated children, let me conclude with the observation that these are the central issues of national educational policy in our time.

Your organization as a whole must address itself to them and so must its smaller units. If American citizens are well informed about the issues, I have no fear of the solutions they will devise.

# CHAPTER 18

## FIRST-RATE CITIES,
## FIRST-RATE SCHOOLS

F OR THE last few years, since education became a glamour industry, we
have been assuring the public that "education is everybody's business." Perhaps
my remarks amount to saying that it is
time educators realize that the cities are
*their* business, and that we will never
have first-rate city schools unless we have
first-rate cities.

From an address before a conference on Urban School Planning, Stanford
University, Stanford, California, July 10, 1967.

# FIRST-RATE CITIES, FIRST-RATE SCHOOLS

Some time ago, a young lady was arrested for posing nude on the steps of J. P. Morgan & Company in New York's financial district, and charged with corrupting the public morals. She was later acquitted because, as her defense attorney pointed out, there was nobody around for several blocks to *be* corrupted.

You may wonder why I open this discussion of the problems of city schools with such an engaging but seemingly irrelevant story. Partly it is to get your attention. Every red-blooded American male has an interest in financial affairs, so I knew that mention of Wall Street would interest you.

But I tell this humble tale also because it seems to me a parable of what is wrong with our cities and their schools. In the past the lamp of learning has symbolized the entire knowledge enterprise, and the shiny red apple has served us as a symbol for American schools in general. It seems to me the young lady clad only in her birthday suit might be an appropriate symbol for our city schools. Why? I'll explain later.

First, I would like to summarize some of the issues that confront city schools and the ways these issues are reflected in school administration.

Our cities and city schools have been saddled with a disproportionate amount of responsibility for what are really state or national problems. At the same time, the power of the cities to solve or even to ameliorate those problems has decreased. The source of these opposing pressures—increasing responsibility, decreasing ability—is not so much population growth as it is population *shift*.

Chicago offers a good illustration of the distinction. Between 1940 and 1965, the Chicago metropolitan area population increased about 44 percent, from 4.5 million people to 6.5 million. However, only about 3 percent of that increase took place within the city limits; the rest occurred in the suburbs.

Normally a major city would find little difficulty in accommodating a 3 percent population growth. It is the *nature* of that growth which heightened Chicago's problems—the problems of the city and of its schools.

In that same 25-year period, Chicago's white population declined by 600,000 while its Negro population increased by nearly 700,000. Against that shift we must put the fact that because of racial discrimination in rights of citizens, in employment, and in educational opportunities, a disproportionate percentage of low-income families in America are Negro families. Thus in 1964, while the median income for white families in the United States was $6,858, the median income for non-white families was $3,839, or only 56 percent of the white income.

The experience of Chicago can be duplicated in greater or less degree in every major American city. The facts and statistics of urban blight, of large racially isolated minorities, of inadequate services to improve the opportunities of Americans who have missed the American dream are all too familiar.

The important thing is what these facts and numbers mean. They mean that better-educated, higher-income families are leaving the city and being replaced by white and Negro families. A high percentage of these families are immigrants from the rural South, with poor educations and low incomes—in some cases, with no education or income of their own at all. More importantly they mean that schools and hospitals, welfare departments and recreation agencies, job training enterprises and employment offices must rethink their purposes and their programs. Since the basic opportunity for change lies in preventing the coming generation from being trapped in the ghetto, the great hope for the future of the American city lies in the city's public schools.

Urban education today must be of a kind radically different from the sort of education American schools have traditionally offered. Although educators have been saying as much for more than a decade, it is only in the last few years that the nation as a whole has come to understand the effects of a deprived home environment on scholastic achievement. It is only in the last few years we have come to realize that the home does much more educating, for better or worse, than any number of teachers can do in six hours a day, five days a week—with three months out for a vacation spent in the summer school of the streets.

As has often been remarked, American schools evolved from white, middle-class, Anglo-Saxon Protestant ideas about what ought to be taught and about what children should want to learn. These ideas work reasonably well when the lessons of the school are reinforced by the lessons of the home. But because these ideas and the assumptions on which they are based are so alien to the lives of millions of disadvantaged urban children today, there is a vast psychological distance between the clientele of today's city schools—the students and their parents—and the suppliers of education: teachers, administrators, and school board members.

This psychological gap reveals itself in a number of ways. One is in a high dropout rate, stemming in large part from the inability of many students to see any connection between their studies and their lives. The most dramatic effect of this psychological distance, however, is the violence we have come to fear and expect in our cities. Usually it has been an arrest or a shooting that has triggered days of rioting or looting, but the apparent cause is so trivial in comparison with the appalling result—in such places as Watts, Chicago, Atlanta, Buffalo, Cleveland, and others—that we must seek explanations elsewhere.

Schooling that results in not learning to read, in not mastering a saleable skill, and in not learning the habits which will lead to job success is certainly one of these causes. I suspect that much of this violence really amounts to a ghetto version of a PTA meeting. Poorly educated parents and poorly educated teenagers, who do not know how to reach a city hierarchy separated from them by a host of cultural differences, seize the only means of communication readily available to them. Riots are an expensive way to talk, but white people are finally listening after decades of ignoring the quieter voices from the ghetto. Officials in city hall and in the board of education offices are now seeking to respond to needs which have been pointed out so forcibly that they cannot be ignored. With assistance from federal programs, they have made a start on problems which have been coming to a head for 100 years. Surely many of them must feel inadequate to the task, just as federal officials like myself do. This feeling of inadequacy stems not from any intention of public officials to do as little as they can get away with but from our genuine inability to understand what has gone wrong and what is needed to make things right. Those in government and those who are supposed to benefit from government have not understood each other.

Closing the gap between city schools and the children they serve will call for vast expenditures of energy, imagination, and money. Urban education is more expensive than suburban or rural education for a number of reasons: Land and construction costs are greater; salaries must be higher to attract teachers into the cities; and where culturally deprived children are concerned, their education must be more expensive because the school is called on to perform much of the instructional work that normally takes place—or should—in the home. These factors taken together obviously place a heavy responsibility on city school personnel to devise a new and more effective brand of education.

But school officials by themselves cannot solve the problem of the city schools, for this problem is not simply educational in nature. It is civic. If we are ever to have fine city schools drawing their strength from the cities themselves, rather than from desperate experiments financed by foundations and federal programs, we must restore to the cities the financial and political power to solve the problems thrust upon them. And we must restore the city neighborhood.

In part, that means attracting back to the cities large numbers of the middle-income families who have moved to the suburbs in the last decade. Many of them, I suspect, would be happy to return. They don't *enjoy* driving two hours a day to work and back; they don't *enjoy* struggling to find a parking place and paying a high price for it when they do. Many of them, I suspect, don't *enjoy* contributing a large portion of their weekend hours to stamping out crabgrass and replacing the furnace filter. And above all, many of them miss the variety which is preeminently the gift of the cities. Suburbs, after all, draw from the city their major reason for being; take away the city with its jobs and its attractions and all you have in the suburbs is a lot of land that might better be put to farming.

The fact is that the cities have sapped their own political power by driving away middle-income families; they have eroded their own financial power through poor land use, unplanned development, and subsidized ugliness. A man with two or three children, an annual income of $10,000, and a normal desire for decent housing cannot afford to live anywhere *but* the suburbs. More and more, the only people who can afford city living are the rich, the poor, and the childless.

In the meantime, our cities blanket some of the most desirable land in the United States—land close to the center of the city—with slum buildings and tracts reserved for automobiles. I understand that fully 50 percent of the Los Angeles downtown area is monopolized by streets and parking lots; in Atlanta, 54 percent; in Boston, 40 percent; in Denver, 44 percent.

What has this kind of thing to do with the city schools?

First of all, it suggests that the cities—especially the older ones, which are prohibited from further expansion by suburban boundaries—have in the past wasted the most valuable financial resource they have: their land. By making better use of it, they can not only make the city a more attractive place to live, but they can generate the extra tax revenues needed to provide first-rate education for all their citizens. It suggests that they can make of themselves genuinely integrated societies with a good, healthy cross section of economic and social classes, each person choosing the kind of housing he wants. And it suggests, too, the feasibility of a new partnership between the cities and private business. Not even the local, state, and federal governments put together can provide the huge sums needed to renovate all of our cities and all of city education. But the cities themselves could do a major share of the job if they harnessed the profit motive to their own goals and matched it with the significant support available from federal sources.

As a start in this direction, cities will have to talk their state legislatures into allowing them to alter the present structure of property taxes. Present property taxes are based mainly on the value of a building, not on the value of the land it occupies. In essence, this approach considers the value of the building to the owner, not to the city, and does not take into consideration the desirability of the land and its location—sometimes called the "site-value"—at all. This approach confuses property taxes with income taxes.

Its result is to discourage the improvement of valuable land close to the center of the city. It is more profitable for a slum landlord to let his aging tenement sit and decay, while he pays low taxes on the building and the site, rather than develop the site or sell it to a private builder who will. The city pays in several ways: through the loss of the tax revenue that good housing or commercial construction on that site would bring; through the loss of middle-income families who might both live and work there; and, finally, through the excessive prices cities must pay for underassessed slum land to convert it to better use. To quote from the report of a conference of 33 urban experts as published in the April 1967 issue of *Nation's Cities,* "Nearly a third of all the people of Manhattan still live in railroad flats that were banned before 1900, and these slums are so underassessed and undertaxed that it has cost an average of $486,000 an acre to buy them up for demolition!"

By now, I hope it will not seem odd to any of you that an educator should spend so much time discussing the use of land and the structure of taxation. For the last few years, since education became a glamour industry, we have been assuring the public that "education is everybody's business." Perhaps my remarks amount to saying that it is time educators realize that the cities are *their* business, and that we will never have first-rate city schools unless we have first-rate cities.

Educators must start paying attention to some matters we have neglected in the past: to tax policy, to site selection, to the multiple use of land and building. We should, now and then, forget about computer-assisted instruction and team teaching and nongraded classes and dream a little bit, not about what kind of city *school* we want but about what kind of *city* we want.

We might dream, for example, not about an education park but about a living park: a building that would integrate retail stores, banks, a medical center, restaurants, offices, and apartments; a building that would not only house and employ people but would at the same time educate their youngsters from preschool through high school.

Think what a natural dent we could make in big-city segregation—racial, social, and economic—if instead of having a bus driver bringing 50 children to school, their own fathers and working mothers brought them to the office. The children of bankers, dentists, secretaries, butchers, elevator operators, accountants—black and white, rich and poor, blue collar and white collar—all going to school in the same place.

And a school, moreover, receiving the benefits of an enlightened tax policy—a policy which would tax central city land in such a way that high-income business properties would replace low-income slums. Such a school would be part of a school system which could afford to surround the building with recreation space, sponsor a community orchestra, organize a Little League. It would exist in the midst of the business and cultural life of the city; while training people to serve the one, it would enrich the lives of its students with the other. It would be open day and night to serve both children and adults. It might be called an "education park," although the image that phrase conjures up has developed overtones the city school should avoid.

For some reason, the popular concept of the education park has come to be a massive structure just about like the schools we have now but enrolling 10,000 children in order to achieve a combination of efficiency and integration. The fact is, however, that the idea of an education park makes no sense at all unless it provides each child with a totally new set of opportunities not found in the school he now has:

• Opportunity for facilities which would be impossibly expensive to place in separate, smaller schools.

• Opportunity for programs requiring highly specialized teachers not available in sufficient numbers to staff all schools, and for courses which attract relatively so few students as to make them impractical for most medium-sized schools.

• Opportunity for services in health, recreation, counseling, job placement, education of the handicapped, and other areas, most of which are neglected altogether or only partially provided in the usual school.

• Opportunity for community involvement in the school and the school's involvement in the community, so that the student uses the school as a bridge to the city and the city becomes his classroom, with all the variety it has to offer.

• Opportunity for parent use of school facilities and for enlisting parents in the cause of the education of their children.

Any school which achieves these objectives will not be the usual kind of school. It will reach out to the best in the city rather than lock its doors against the worst at 3:30 in the afternoon. It will find ways within a much enlarged student body to give each youngster the feeling that he belongs and that somebody knows his name. Without being a neighborhood school in the traditional sense, it will create an atmosphere of neighborhood in the city which does not exist there now. Such a school may be three miles long and 300 yards wide, as was recently suggested for a portion of New York City. Or it may be 60 stories high and integrated with business and dwelling facilities. Whatever the formulation, it will be different in every city, because every city has a different history, a different population mix, a different relationship to its suburbs and to its state government, and different resources of money and imagination. And whatever the formulation of the city school of the future, it will depend on more than the planning of educators.

Educators must think about buildings and transportation and air pollution while they forge new alliances with city planners, architects, politicians and precinct captains, industrialists and chain store operators, and all the people who make a city go. We must, in brief, form a new integration of specialties, for it is, above all, *dis*integration that threatens both cities and schools today. Our cities tend to enforce the segregation of minority from majority, of rich from poor, and to separate us in all the aspects of our lives. We drive 20 miles from the place we work to the place we play. We have allowed expressways, urban growth, and suburban sprawl to distribute our lives into cubicles separated from each other by concrete, dirty air, dirty water, and political boundaries that encourage apathy. Our schools and offices, busy while the sun shines, become blacked-out warehouses when work is over. Our theaters, our imposing monuments to culture, do not come alive *until* dark. And our downtown areas, comprising billions of dollars of physical and spiritual investment, millions of humans working with an imagination and energy that have amazed the world, are ghost towns from five at night until nine in the morning, and all day Saturday and Sunday.

Nobody's around. The ticking of the clock ends one part of a person's daily life, signals the start of another, and tells him it's time to go someplace else.

What are we to think of a young lady who takes her clothes off in the middle of Wall Street?

As a federal official, I think her conduct was scandalous, immoral, and reprehensible.

As a private citizen with something resembling 20-20 vision, I kind of wish I had been around to be corrupted.

But as both a public and a private citizen with an interest in education, I think we ought to wonder why nobody *was* there. Because if we do not, one day we may find that what was true of Wall Street on one Sunday in New York will be permanently true of one great city after another, and of one city school after another: nobody's there.

# TEACHING FOR THE FUTURE

T HE POINT is that there is a new sense
of experimentation in education today, a receptive attitude toward fresh
ideas, a willingness to try those approaches which promise to make schooling more interesting and more effective.
Much of this experimentalism in the
search for a better way to teach or for
more important matters to teach about
has been made possible by the appropriations of the Congress.

---

Summer commencement address, Northeast Missouri State Teachers College,
Kirksville, Missouri, August 10, 1967.

---

# TEACHING FOR THE FUTURE

THE PRESIDENT OF YOUR COLLEGE TELLS ME THAT nearly 90 percent of you are headed out into the wide world as teachers. That being the case, I hope the rest of you will not take it amiss if I devote most of my remarks today to the subject of teaching. Even if you do not plan to make a career of education, I think most of you will find, sooner or later, that teaching concerns you very much. You will compare notes with the young couple supporting the mortgage next to yours, find that their ten-year-old is already on the Civil War while yours is still perched on Plymouth Rock, and you will charge into the next PTA meeting loaded for bear.

Such are the hazards of being a teacher. Fortunately, the rewards are starting to catch up with the risks. Perhaps the most obvious measure is economic. A century ago, when both Northeast Missouri and the U. S. Office of Education were founded, American teachers earned an average of $180 a year. Today the average is up to about $6,000, enough to enable the average teacher to qualify for charge accounts and bank loans and, in short, to go as heavily into debt as any other citizen.

There are other ways to measure the American teacher's slow climb to full citizenship. Within a few months after you enter a school system, you will probably be invited to join one or the other of two national teachers' associations—the National Education Association or the American Federation of Teachers. I will not attempt to describe the differences between the two, since I will undoubtedly slight one or both, and I am not anxious to get into a tangle with either. The NEA and the AFT could, between them, muster more indignant letters than I care to answer.

The basic point to be made about the NEA and the AFT is that the competition between them, as well as the activities of each, has altered the status of American teachers rather strikingly in the last decade. Until about the middle 1950's, teachers tended to be nearly anonymous, performing their jobs with devotion and imagination, but nonetheless working under conditions dictated almost exclusively by local school boards. They had relatively little voice in determining such matters as teacher salaries, the number of students to be assigned to a classroom, the reasons for which a teacher could be dismissed from his job, or, in some schools at least, the content of the curriculum.

Today a new militancy among teachers is making school superintendents, school boards, and even mayors sit up and pay attention to those to whom we entrust the education of our children. Although men of good will can differ about the propriety of their demands and the methods used to reinforce them, I count it as a gain that teachers today can speak up as free men and women. The teaching environment has improved in the last decade, and it will improve more. You are entering a profession which has a growing influence on policy through the collective action of its members. As you move into responsible roles in that profession, you have the obligation to use this newfound power as much for the benefit of the children you will teach as for the benefit of yourselves.

But perhaps the greatest appeal in being a teacher today is that the job itself is so much more interesting. In the last ten years we have witnessed a genuine revolution in American education. I use that word despite the fact that TV advertisers have nearly drained it of meaning through repetition. The word *revolution* means a turning-over, a flip-flop in the established way of doing things. We have seen such a turning-over in American education in the last ten years.

For one thing, we have seen it in the rapid development of

a national role for the federal government in education. Until very recent times, the only educational function of the federal government was to stay out of the way, letting the states and the local school districts run the schools and pay for them.

For many years, there has been a sort of national consensus that every American child had the right to a high school education at public expense, but this was not a consensus agreed upon or enacted by the federal government. It is easy to take this consensus for granted, and to forget what a struggle went into its establishment. A predecessor of mine—the first Commissioner of Education, as a matter of fact—was one of the earliest advocates of free public schools. His proposal was regarded as so radical in the 1830's and 1840's that a Rhode Island farmer threatened to shoot him. But over a period of years, every state accepted the idea until now it is inconceivable that a state should not provide free public schools. And yet there is no national law requiring them to do so.

In a sense, therefore, we have not had until recently a national policy in education—and I am not entirely sure that we have one now. But we do have a totally different degree of participation in education by the national government. What is revolutionary is the role now being played by the people's representatives in Congress in shaping federal participation in education—in identifying basic contributions the schools can make to our national economic and social progress, and coming up with the money to help them do it.

Now if your political views run in a conservative direction, you may equate federal aid to education as "control," or at least as a form of bribery: Washington holding out the carrot and telling the states and their local systems they can have it only by going in the direction the federal government wants them to go. Actually, however, it would be difficult to imagine a better way for our national legislative body to address itself to national problems without conflicting with local prerogatives.

What Congress has done in the last ten years is to maintain the traditional and constitutional freedom of the states in education while recognizing that poor education in any state weakens the entire nation. In 1958, when the Russians sent up Sputnik and damaged the national ego of a people accustomed to being first, we realized that scientific and technical education in the United States badly needed improvement. Although some schools had first-rate laboratories, plenty of equipment, and well-trained teacher-scientists, many did not. Whatever our national needs or goals, the quality of science instruction in the United States depended on the unrelated decisions of thousands of local school boards and on the amount of taxes local citizens were willing or able to levy on themselves.

Here was an area where state and local freedom *could* conflict with the national interest. Just as there is no law requiring states to establish schools in the first place, so there is no law requiring any state to teach physics or chemistry in the schools it does maintain. Yet it was obviously essential to the security and the scientific progress of the United States that we have numbers of well-educated physicists, chemists, biologists, and technicians of a dozen sorts. Congress could not order the states to make a sound, basic scientific education available to every youngster who wanted one but it could appropriate money for that purpose and offer it to the states. Congress did so, under the National Defense Education Act of 1958. In effect this Act took our national policy in education one step farther. It said, simply, that the people of the United States recognized that education in certain broad fields was sufficiently important to the nation as a whole to require federal aid when local school districts could not adequately finance such instruction by themselves.

During the years since 1958, Congress has passed more laws to support education than all the previous Congresses clear back to 1787, when the first Congress met. And each law has more fully defined the idea of a national interest in education while at the same time safeguarding the preeminence of the states, localities, and independent institutions in operating the schools and colleges.

Thus in 1963, through the Higher Education Facilities Act, Congress recognized that the "baby boom" of the post-World War II years was about to hit our colleges and universities and that there weren't enough classroom seats for everyone who could benefit from a higher education. In 1965, through the Elementary and Secondary Education Act, Congress recognized that throughout the country, the quality of a youngster's education depended heavily on where he was born—and that, in so many cases as to constitute a serious national problem, the level of quality was low because local government lacked the resources to support education as they should. This was particularly true of education for the children of deprived families; such education costs more per child because it must make up for the shortcomings of the youngster's home and neighborhood. That same year, through the Higher Education Act of 1965, Congress recognized that our colleges and universities could help to solve the problems of our cities if they were given the necessary resources, just as state universities have in the past conducted research on agricultural problems and helped make the American farmer the most productive in the world. In the same Act, Congress gave support for the strengthening of college libraries and for the improvement of those institutions with the capacity to change, and it made new commitments to training teachers for the schools.

Each of these pieces of legislation has helped shape a new role for the federal government in education. Broadly stated, that role boils down to the proposition that Congress and the Administration are using education as a tool for working on important national problems: to combat poverty and unemployment; to reverse the decline of our cities; to improve our ability to handle international responsibilities through supporting instruction in foreign language and area studies; to maintain the pace of our national life through the support of artists and scholars whose contributions cannot be measured in increased productivity or strengthened military defense.

In effect, the years from 1958 until now have seen the federal government make increasing use of education as the means for building into each individual the capacity to solve his own problems and to contribute to the welfare of others.

The new federal participation in education is of consuming interest to political scientists and historians. What difference does it make to the individual teacher, to his career prospects, to the sort of professional life he can look forward to, to those who are graduating today?

First, it means that teachers have new financial and physical resources to help them do the things they know ought to be done to help children. It means that their students have more textbooks, more microscopes, more metal-turning lathes, more of the tools of learning. It means that teacher aides can take over more of the routine classroom chores, thus freeing the teacher to do the professional work he was hired to do. It means that teachers themselves have more opportunity to improve their professional skills through federally supported graduate study or institutes at colleges and universities across the country.

But perhaps most important, the maturing of our national interest in education has breathed a new life, a new scholarship, and even a new fun into teaching. You have undoubtedly heard of the new math, and perhaps of the new physics. You may not have heard of the new geography, since it has just gotten out of the testing phase. In essence, this is an attempt to bring inductive reasoning to a subject which has too often been a rote process of memorizing the names of capitals and mountain ranges and major exports. The new geography stresses the *why* instead of the *what* or *where*. Just a few weeks ago, a group of faculty members at Princeton University announced that they had begun work on a "new history," and at least one major educational publisher has brought out a grammatical approach being billed as the "new English."

By citing these developments, I do not mean to say that they are all superior to the old methods, nor even that they are as good. I frankly don't know enough about some of them to offer an opinion. The point is that there is a new sense of experimentation in education today, a receptive attitude toward fresh ideas, a willingness to try those approaches which promise to make schooling more interesting and more effective. Much of this experimentalism in the search for a better way to teach or for more important matters to teach about has been made possible by the appropriations of the Congress.

Here in Kirksville, for example, 60 local youngsters will benefit from Project Follow Through. As you may know, Follow Through is an extension of Operation Head Start which has been so successful in helping culturally deprived children make up for the poor family backgrounds which can hamper them in their later school work. The Kirksville project is designed to insure that the gains achieved by these youngsters under Head Start are not lost as they leave preschool and begin kindergarten. It combines kindergarten instruction with auxiliary services such as medical and dental care—so-called "frills" which nevertheless have a direct bearing on scholastic achievement.

This, again, is an example of the new spirit in American education—a readiness to tinker with the traditional way of doing things to see if a new idea can improve routine practice. Those of you who go into teaching will benefit from this new spirit in a very direct way. Because the American teacher has stopped being passive and has started reaching for a share in directing the progress of education, your energies and ideas will have much more influence than they would have ten years ago. That means that you will have a much better chance of finding personal fulfillment in education, a much better chance for building a career that promises both spiritual and material rewards.

The new spirit in American schools will also benefit those of you who are *not* going into teaching, in that it promises to give your children a better education than either your generation or mine received.

Finally, this new spirit will make this nation and this world better places to live in. It may seem difficult to reconcile that statement with the frightening and appalling events we have witnessed in our cities in the past several weeks. It must seem sometimes that every advance in social reform achieved by local, state, and federal governments triggers new expressions of resentment in our city ghettoes, rather than producing measurable progress in racial harmony. And the temptation, in turn, is to assume that these social programs have failed, and that we might as well stop pouring tax money into them.

To my mind, this would be a fatal conclusion. There is no need for me to recite here the centuries-long history of American injustice to the American Negro, nor to point out that we are 100 years late in delivering the guarantees of equal citizenship under law extended by the Thirteenth, Fourteenth, and Fifteenth Amendments to the Consitituion. Justice delayed is justice denied, and we have a great deal of ground to make up.

You are becoming teachers at a time when our schools are in the front lines of social change and social progress. With the aid of the federal government, public schools across the land have within very recent years addressed themselves to achieving success with those children who are hardest to teach, who come to school least prepared in every way for what schools expect of them. You are part of the new generation of teachers who will use the new resources of education to lead these disadvantaged young people into the light. A large proportion of them are Negroes; your generation of teachers must find the way to bring them self-respect in an America not yet fully committed to meeting its promises.

And at this point in time, educated Americans—black and white—must above all retain their nerve, their intellectual stamina, and their determination not to allow stupidity, black or white, to impede the social reform to which we committed ourselves 100 years ago. Above all, we must remember that the current American program of social reform is not rooted in a vague desire to be nice, but in a hard-minded, clear-eyed recollection that this nation was founded to safeguard liberty and justice for *all*. Just as every one of us has benefited from the sacrifices of earlier Americans who defended and enlarged our freedoms, both in war and peace, so it is our turn now to forge a better homeland for millions of fellow citizens whom we shall never see.

The future has its roots in today. As college graduates, it is not only your privilege, but it is also your responsibility, to insure that we shall all have a better tomorrow.

# CHAPTER 20

# PEERING ACROSS THE GENERATION GAP

O NE's 30TH birthday neither guarantees wisdom nor prevents it. On
just about any issue you can name—
civil rights, Vietnam, the draft, use of
drugs, perhaps even all-digit-dialing—I
suspect you could enlist as many allies
from beyond the 30th parallel as from
your side of it.

---

From an address before the Annual National Conference, National Student
Association, College Park, Maryland, August 22, 1967.

---

# PEERING ACROSS THE GENERATION GAP

ITHAS BECOME A COMMONPLACE OF CONFRONTA-
tions like this for the middle-aged speaker to genuflect a few times
in the direction of the "Generation Gap." This is, of course, the
abyss that separates clear-eyed youth such as yourselves from
myoptic, battle-worn old-timers like me.

I have spent a fair amount of time brooding over this gap—
ever since I first saw one of those lapel buttons that read, "Don't
Trust Anyone Over 30." That stark injunction hurt. Some of my
best friends are over 30—nearly *all* of them, as a matter of fact.
And they seem to me a decent lot—happy and courteous and
fun loving. Why, then, should the vociferous members of your
generation repudiate this splendid crew of my generation?

The answer, of course, is that no intelligent person of any age
makes this kind of blanket rejection. One's 30th birthday neither
guarantees wisdom nor prevents it. On just about any issue you
can name—civil rights, Vietnam, the draft, use of drugs, perhaps
even all-digit-dialing—I suspect you could enlist as many allies
from beyond the 30th parallel as from your side of it.

This is not to deny, however, that there is such a thing as a
generation gap. I am convinced there is; moreover, I believe it is
an aggravated phenomenon of our time, a difference in outlook
that divides your contemporaries from mine in a way that we
were never separated from *our* elders.

In my view, the new Generation Gap consists mainly of an
early maturing which has led your generation to start worrying
about the large problems of our society at a much earlier age than

*my* contemporaries did. And after taking a quick look around, many of you have decided that in several respects my generation has botched the job of running our world. Speaking as a witness for the defense, I don't agree. We've had problems that Martin Van Buren and Chester Alan Arthur wouldn't *believe*. Risking your ire a little further, I'd say that I don't think you will amaze the world when it comes time for *you* to conduct American foreign and domestic affairs.

On the other hand, I believe much of your criticism is well founded; my generation deserves a lot of lumps for our fumbling and often tardy efforts to handle problems we might have spotted 10 or 20 years ago. Moreover, I hope that you will retain your sharpness of view and tongue after you move into the full responsibilities of adult, tax-paying, child-raising citizenship. Your early dissent augurs well for the future of our country, for the day will come when you yourselves will become the Establishment, despite the baleful feelings some of you have about the present Establishment and anybody connected with it.

Looking toward that day, I am tempted to manufacture some quickie wisdom on a dozen subjects which I think you ought to consider. Unfortunately for my ego, the complexity of the problems that cross my desk force me to question whether I am competent to advise anybody about anything. This doubt, I might add, is shared by some members of Congress. One of them got up in the House of Representatives a while ago and said that "The Commissioner of Education is so ignorant he ought to incorporate. No one," he said, "should own so much of one commodity."

Rather than offer advice, therefore, I will restrict myself to some thoughts about just two subjects: one of which you are doubtless interested in—you; and another that you ought to be interested in—our cities. There are those who think both you and the cities are out of control. Whether they are out of control or not, they have some connection with each other. Not only will you live or work in or near the cities, but what you do about them may determine the future more than any of us realizes.

The age of geographical exploration on our planet has very nearly vanished. The adventurous members of your generation must seek frontiers elsewhere either in space or in what seem to me the more profound and demanding explorations of human possibility here on earth. And whatever form your quest for self-fulfillment takes—whether it be a forthright desire to make a million dollars or an altruistic itch to give at least one other human being a hand when he most needs it—I think each of you could find in our cities an arena for your efforts.

Some of you have already discovered this, as students in those of our urban universities which have begun to tackle the problems of that larger campus which lies beyond the college gate. Opportunities to test your mettle are being created daily as both private and public bodies search for ways to reverse the decline of our cities. Among federal programs, for example, I could cite VISTA—Volunteers in Service to America—or the Teacher Corps, both of which I would urge you to investigate and consider.

These and similar programs represent what I might call "points of entry," attempts to grasp the tangled threads of poor education, unemployment, and low income to see if a tug here or a tug there will help unravel the knot. Because the factors which maintain the city ghetto as a place of spiritual and material poverty are so interrelated, it is difficult to know where to start. Certainly no one program is going to provide the answer. And because our human and material resources for dealing with urban problems are limited, we must carefully weigh a variety of possible investments to see which ones offer the greatest possible return.

In connection with this sort of appraisal, I was most interested to note a recent Labor Department statement that nearly half of the people living in the typical urban slum are less than 18 years old. If that be so, it is clear that to make our cities viable we must make a huge investment in education—not only of dollars, but of ideas, of experiments in providing much more effective education than our ghettoes have had so far.

The great debate about remedying the defects of inner-city schools centers around two broad notions. The first is the radical improvements in education to serve ghetto pupils where they are, even if they are segregated. This is sometimes called "compensatory education." The second is the desegregation of ghetto schools to prevent them from perpetuating the evils of a segregated society.

I think that the participants in this debate have at least chosen the two topics on which we ought to focus if we really intend to develop in ghetto children the capacity to build decent lives for themselves. The problem is that the debaters are choosing up sides, acting as if we must try compensatory education *or* school desegregation but can't move toward both.

As is suggested by the term, compensatory education tries to compensate—to make up for disadvantages the ghetto child brings to school with him by making his schools particularly good schools, sensitive to his needs and committed to developing his potentialities.

The typical white or Negro child from a middle-income home enters kindergarten or first grade with a kind of head start on the learning process. The ghetto child seldom has this advantage. Rarely has he handled a book of any description; often he has never even had a chance to mark up a piece of paper with a pencil. He enters a strange and alien place when he walks into his first classroom; he is subjected to a strange discipline and asked to do unfamiliar things.

In 1965 James Coleman of Johns Hopkins and Ernest Campbell of Vanderbilt directed a survey of more than 600,000 school children for the Office of Education. Their report is the most comprehensive study anyone has ever made of American schools, and we have just begun to distill its many findings into policies that will improve our educational system.

Two findings from the study are particularly relevant to any strategy for improving ghetto schools. One indicates that far from helping students overcome cultural handicaps, ghetto schools maintain the gap in scholastic achievement between children from low-income homes and those from more fortunate families. After a ghetto child has been in school six years, he is about a year and a half behind his middle-income peers in reading achievement. By ninth grade, he has fallen two and a half years behind, and after 12 years of school, he is more than three years behind in the normal measures of scholastic attainment.

These findings make a strong argument for the importance of compensatory education. They show that thinking of equality in education in terms of equal financial investment is really nonsense. Performance *is* partially a matter of environment; if it takes $750 a year to give a surburban youngster a good education, it may well take $1,500 to provide a ghetto child with an equivalent opportunity to develop his abilities through schooling.

Another finding of the report that I want to call to your attention today was startling, rather than shocking. Researchers found that the greatest single factor influencing a student's performance was his attitude toward himself, his own estimate of his chances for succeeding in life. Moreover, this attitude depended to a significant degree on the attitudes of the other children in his class.

Simply stated, this finding means that it does make a difference *whom you go to school with*. It means that if you live in a ghetto where almost nobody goes to college, where most of the fathers have menial jobs or none at all, where there simply are no examples of success on display—you have relatively little chance of visualizing success for yourself or of seeing school as an avenue to self-realization. Summing up this particular conclusion, the report stated:

. . . The responses of pupils to questions in the survey show that minority pupils, except for Orientals, have far less conviction than whites that they can affect their own environments and futures. . . .

Furthermore, while this characteristic shows little relationship to most school factors, it is related, for Negroes, to the proportion of whites in the schools.

And this, I need hardly point out, is a strong argument for school desegregation. It suggests that compensatory education, essential as it is in making up for the defects of a deprived family background, will not by itself turn the trick. For compensatory education does not touch the psychological isolation to which racial discrimination subjects the American Negro. We cannot hope to convince the Negro child that he is as good as any other youngster as long as we quarantine him in schools reserved for racial and national minorities.

On the other side of the argument, we cannot expect school desegregation by itself to give minority children an equal chance to compete with their classmates from the white majority. Integration without special efforts to provide for the special educational needs of all the children involved in it may be a *step* in the right direction. But we must find ways to work on school integration and school improvement at the same time. Difficult as this dual and sometimes contradictory task is, my generation is fortunate in having some remarkable tools to help us accomplish it—tools handed us by President Johnson and the Congress of the United States. In less than four years as chief executive, President Johnson has delivered more legislation on behalf of education than all previous presidents combined.

For example, in just one crucial area—education of culturally deprived children—the Office of Education and the Office of Economic Opportunity alone administer $2 billion in federal funds aimed at reaching and teaching the children of poverty. This is more than the entire *nation* spent to operate *all* its public elementary and high schools in 1940, when my generation sat where yours does now. And even this $2 billion total excludes funds from other federal departments—Housing and Urban Development, Labor, Justice—which directly and indirectly improve the environment in which these children mature.

There is no question that more money is needed to help us eliminate the inferior ghetto schools which breed poverty. Yet the most modest attempt at perspective and objectivity compels us to realize that only in recent years have we made a serious start toward upgrading slum schools.

Now let me turn to a topic closer to home—your home. As you have pointed out on numerous campuses of late, the rapid growth of higher education has its drawbacks. Your list of grievances is long, and while I do not always sympathize with your methods for expressing them, I often share your concern.

One of the most pressing problems on today's campus is the second-class status of undergraduate instruction. We should certainly be able to provide a more flexible and personal brand of instruction than is currently available at many universities.

We may find a part of the answer in educational technology. The lecture platform serves as an apt setting for the gifted speaker, for the teacher who can project the enthusiasm and quality of mind with which he approaches his research. But for sheer efficiency in information transmission we might do well to explore the individualized use of video tapes, programed texts, computer-assisted instruction and the like.

Relegating the transmission of facts to a machine frees the teacher to do what he's really good at: leading an intelligent discussion in an area of knowledge of interest to both him and his students. Whether such discussion follows the lines of the ages, the old Socratic dialogue, or whether it takes such more contemporary forms as simulation or "game," it puts the teacher back where he belongs—in personal contact with his students.

Of course, as the psychologists have shown, behavior is partly determined by rewards and punishments. Thus, one of my concerns is the development of a reward system for quality research. But in order to reward quality teaching, we must first be able to identify it. Toward that end the Office of Education recently gave a grant to your National Student Association to support Project SCATE, a program designed to encourage and develop new student-based methods of teacher and course evaluation.

Although some of my peers feel that students already have too much say in higher education, I think we would do well to examine the active and constructive role students are playing in shaping their colleges and universities. Old Westbury, the new experimental college in the State University of New York system, has recruited students from all over the country to aid in its planning. Last year the College of the University of

Chicago included students in a week-long conference to assess its educational goals. We have a small group of students at the Office of Education this summer working on research needs in higher education.

In some cases, students have also tried their hand at creating new *forms* of education. The Free University Movement at San Francisco State College has spread to more than 60 college campuses and communities. Their course offerings are intriguing: Non-Violence in a Violent World, Black Writers, Dance of Joy, Obscure Literature, Sex Education for a Changing Society, and Technology and Human Emotions.

Whether or not these experiments succeed, they will at least broaden our thinking about higher education. Rising costs, burgeoning enrollments, teacher shortages, technological change, and the knowledge explosion have made many of our current practices obsolete. Despite our national pride in diversity, a surprising "sameness" permeates most of American higher education. At a time when the public schools are realizing the importance of individual differences and are adopting individualized instruction, independent study, flexible scheduling, team teaching, nongraded classes, and similar practices, most colleges and universities still subscribe to a uniform four-year, 125-unit system.

It is time we took a critical look at such old standards as the four-year baccalaureate (why four? why not two, or six, or ten?), the residency requirement (why not a couple of years with the Peace Corps in Ethiopia or with VISTA in Chicago?), the "A" to "F" grading system (why not more sophisticated evaluation with *real* validity?), the 50-minute lecture and the semester-long course (why not more flexible learning units varying from two minutes to two years?), the discipline-oriented curriculum (why not curricula which revolve around such problems as poverty, or peace, or urban planning?).

Another large area noticeable by its absence is a rational, informed concern for student growth in that somewhat frightening and highly personal matter of feelings and emotions.

Whether this calls for new educational programs or can be handled largely by a more sophisticated attitude on the part of college and university administrations, I don't know. I do believe that faculty and administrations must recognize the profound influence their attitudes toward students have on emotional and personal development. It makes a great difference, for example, whether a college president regards a sharp manifestation of student dissent as a revolt of the palace serfs, to be put down as rapidly and quietly as possible, or as a legitimate protest from full citizens of the academic community who are entitled to be heard and negotiated with—not just dealt with.

Now, lest it seem to my peers that I've sold out to your generation, let me say that I find some of your causes and activities disturbing. I am deeply concerned, for example, about the increasing use of drugs on our major campuses; it is clearly time we mounted a major program of drug education—not propaganda—for your generation *and for mine*. My generation needs to understand that a combination of preaching and rigid discipline won't solve the drug problem; both our generations need a new willingness to engage in an exchange of ideas about that problem.

The reported stifling of free speech by student dissidents is also disturbing. Just as I welcome such statements as that on student rights and freedoms recently drafted by the American Association of University Professors in conjunction with a number of other national education associations, so I would urge you to respect the rights of others to contradict your views. I have *no* respect for students who claim the privileges of academic freedom yet whose actions deny it to others with whom they disagree.

On balance, however, my major concern about student dissidents today is that as you grow older you may lose the sharpness of your viewpoints and the determination to put those viewpoints to work. My boss, Secretary John Gardner, has put this thought in language worth your attention. I want to quote him now:

The young people of this generation are perhaps more alert to the problems of the larger society than any preceding generation. But for all their activism, there is every likelihood that they will follow the familiar trend—a few years of indignant concern for social betterment, characterized by a demand for immediate solutions to all the world's problems, and then a trailing off into the apathy and disinterest of the young executive or professional.

If you want to avoid the toughest problems facing your generation, there are some classic forms of escape. One is to get so wrapped up in your personal life that there just isn't any time for the larger problems of the day. A more subtle exit . . . is to immerse oneself so deeply in a specialized professional field that the larger community virtually ceases to exist . . . Still another and infinitely devious means of turning your back on the larger community is to assert that the whole society is so corrupt that nothing can save it. Such moral gamesmanship relieves the gamesman of all responsibility. With one shrug he shakes off the burden that serious men have carried from the beginning of time, the struggle to make an imperfect society work.

A variation on that theme is to tell yourself that the society has fallen into the hands of unworthy people, and that virtuous, clear-eyed spirits such as yourself haven't a chance. You can suck that lollipop of self-deceit all your life and die secure in the belief that the world would have been different had they turned it over to you.

Unfortunately we can no longer afford such escapism on the part of our best young people. They must lend a hand. In doing so, they will be committing themselves to an arduous assignment.

They will have to be willing to undergo the long, hard apprenticeship that is required to accomplish change in the modern world. It's a complex world. It can't be run by the untrained or changed by the untrained.

And after they're trained they have to have the fortitude and staying power essential to the long, difficult task of accomplishing social change. Making a bad world better is tough, grinding, never-ending work. It's not for people whose chief interest is in posturing or striking an attitude or bandying words or venting the anger of youth.

In concluding this quote from the Secretary, I can only say that I wish I'd said that. And to conclude this speech, I will simply revise one more quotation that has gained currency among your generation: turn on and tune in, but don't drop out.

# CHAPTER 21

# THE STRENGTH OF A SPARROW

WE DESPERATELY need new ideas if we are to solve the financial as well as the social and cultural problems of the cities. There is a very real danger that even if we had twice as much money available to us, these additional funds might make relatively little difference. They might simply be dissipated in doing more of the same.

From an address before the Urban Schools Conference, sponsored by the National School Boards Association and the Office of the Vice President, Washington, D. C., September 22, 1967.

# THE STRENGTH OF
# A SPARROW

THERE IS AN OLD ARABIAN LEGEND ABOUT A SPINDLY little sparrow who was lying on his back in the middle of the road. A horseman came by, dismounted, and asked the sparrow what on earth he was doing lying there upside down like that.

"I heard the heavens were going to fall today," said the sparrow.

"Oh?" said the horseman, "And I suppose you think your puny little bird legs can hold up the heavens?"

"One does what one can," said the sparrow; "one does what one can."

Well, the heavens seem to be falling on our cities, and if we sparrows do what we can, I'm not so sure but what together we can hold up the heavens at that.

First we have to understand why they are falling.

One reason is the social change that is taking place at a rate many Americans find alarming. The story is so familiar that I shall not dwell upon it here. We are stuffed to our eyeballs with data on the pathology of the cities. Instead I would like to talk with you for a few moments about economic change.

For several decades, school board associations have been worrying about the economic problems confronted by suburban school districts—districts that were struggling to house and teach classes that doubled and tripled not only as a consequence of the post-war baby boom but as a consequence also of the flight from the cities to the surrounding bedroom communities. The big question was how these communities, with a tax base composed of dwellings which provide more children than money, could build enough schools and support an adequate educational program. As an answer, school board associations urged state legislatures to equalize the tax burden for suburban property owners.

Today the problem is reversed and it is the city that is in trouble. But state legislatures, locked into the formulas of the 1940's and the 1950's, still give preferential treatment to the suburbs as they apportion their education funds.

A study of 35 cities by Professor Seymour Sacks, reported in *Urban Affairs Quarterly*, shows that the cities averaged $124.92 per pupil in state aid last year, while the suburban districts got an average of $165.54 per student—a difference of $40.62. And to cite a specific example, while the State of Ohio was providing the City of Cleveland with $99 per pupil—pupils outside the eight large metropolitan areas of the state received $161 per pupil.

Such imbalances arise, as you well know, from excessive reliance on a single piece of economic data: the number of dollars of assessed value behind each student in the district. It is time, I think, that we considered more relevant data.

City resources are tapped by a wide range of special municipal services, and this urban "overburden" is rarely given due recognition by the states. I am, of course, referring to the disproportionate expenditures that the cities must make for non-school services—for police and fire protection, for garbage collection, for health and welfare services, for streets and street-lighting, for street cleaning and sewage treatment, for community action programs and public housing and museums and public transit systems—not only for their own residents but for all the commuters who use these services every day without adequately reimbursing the city.

A U. S. Office of Education Cooperative Research Project last year showed that the cities spent an average of 65 percent of their local tax dollars on non-school services, leaving only 35 percent for education. In the non-metropolitan areas, these percentages were reversed. The suburban areas had 65 percent of their funds available for the schools.

For many cities the contrast is even more dramatic. Let me give you a few examples: in the Commonwealth of Pennsylvania, communities outside the metropolitan areas spend only 22 percent of local tax funds on non-school items. The City of Philadelphia spends 58 percent.

In San Francisco, 71 percent of local tax funds are required for non-school items, while the state-wide figure is 49 percent. The figure for New York State is also 49 percent—but the City of Buffalo spends 76 percent on non-school items.

Concurrently, while the demands on the city's services and revenues have been increasing, its tax base has been decreasing as one corporation after another has heeded the siren song of handsome new industrial parks developed in the suburbs.

In Baltimore, for example, the number of tax dollars behind each pupil dropped 19.3 percent during the last five years while the property value per pupil in Maryland's suburbs and rural areas increased by more than 10 percent. In Cleveland the same comparison shows a 10 percent drop in the dollars behind each pupil for the city, while the suburbs and rural areas increased by almost 5 percent. Thus the proportionate amounts of money available to the city schools have been decreasing at the very time that the need for money has been increasing and as educational problems have become more intense.

When families drop out of the city to live in the suburbs they take with them their higher incomes, their middle-class motivation and drive, and the greater cultural exposure they offer their children. One of the results has been a sharp break with the traditional makeup of the American school classroom, a cleavage which concentrates children of economically and culturally deprived families—white and Negro alike—in the central city school, effectively separated from the children of more affluent families.

These city children cost more to educate. How much more? Nobody knows for sure. We can only guess at what it would actually cost to run a topflight city school system. No city in the nation has yet had the funds to do what its authorities would consider a truly effective job.

So if the sky is falling over the cities, if our city schools have been something less than a success, it isn't just because of racial and social inequity. It is also because of fiscal inequity.

My years of involvement with the massive and complex problems of the cities have taught me a good deal of humility. I don't pretend that I have all the answers for you, or that the U. S. Office of Education does. The federal government is a new partner in this task of improving education and we are working hard to make our assistance more effective.

In the financial picture of the schools, we cover only a corner of the canvas. Currently the Office of Education contributes about 8 percent of the total cost of public elementary-secondary education in the United States, with 92 percent coming from the states and local communities. Perhaps one day the federal share will be greater. Conceivably it could double.

Even so dramatic an increase, however, would remain a relatively minor element in the total economics of public education —although this 8 percent looms very large indeed when one considers its purpose and direction. It has two major characteristics. First, it is additional money designed to provide services over and above what states and localities have previously found possible, and second, it is focused on the most pressing educational problems—the culturally deprived child who is headed for failure, the handicapped child who needs special teachers and services, and research necessary to help the schools develop the capacity to successfully confront modern problems.

The contributions of President Johnson and the 89th Congress to American public education, contributions which will be recognized by history, have given schools the leverage to work on vital national challenges to education. The federal government neither can nor should assume the major day-in-and-day-out financial support of the schools. That is a job for the states and the localities, and my contention is that the states are just not doing an adequate job for the cities.

Some state legislatures have begun to recognize the serious misalignment of their tax distribution patterns. Massachusetts rewrote its formula two years ago, and while I gather that there are complaints that real equity has not yet been achieved for the cities, everyone seems to agree there has been progress. New York also established a new formula, and so did Pennsylvania after the Pittsburgh schools mounted a massive campaign to convince the state that the schools were confronting a critical financial crisis. Pennsylvania now provides 35 percent of Pittsburgh's $42 million school budget; in 1964 the city got 23 percent of its budget from the state.

Pittsburgh has enjoyed other successes. The city passed a $50 million bond issue to help finance the Great High Schools Program last year when bond issues were failing like falling dominoes in cities across the country. The exodus of middle-class white families appears to have been halted; some suburban parents have asked if their children could get in the Great Scholars program. (They can, says Pittsburgh Superintendent Sidney Marland—if they move back to Pittsburgh.) Significant numbers of people do not seem to be moving back to Pittsburgh yet—but neither are they leaving.

How did they do it in Pittsburgh?

Part of the answer lies in the fact that the city's appointed Board of Education has demonstrated that its members are responsive to, in close touch with, and have the support of the business community, the minority community, and the intellectual community. The schools, partly by involving dozens of citizens' groups in school planning from the very beginning, have managed to evoke broad public support for excellence in education and for providing the kind of financial support that excellence requires.

I do not mean in these references to Pittsburgh to veer into the issue of appointed school boards vis-a-vis elected boards. The difference in a school board's success in getting community support appears to lie less in the mechanics of selection than in the prestige attached to school board membership: that phenomenon that builds a tradition by which service on the school board, whether by appointment or election, becomes the business of the community's most distinguished citizens.

If your city has no such tradition, it is high time to get about establishing one. You'll have to start by persuading the people who occupy suites at the top of the skyscrapers to become involved with what's going on down there in the streets. Such people, I would suppose, are more ready than most to perceive the essential role of education in halting the erosion of the cities. Moreover, they have the potential of being education's warmest advocates. Their political and economic muscle forms a resource that city schools can ill afford to do without.

Another vital step is to enlarge our view of the role of the schools—to cease looking upon them as special purpose islands in the city, separated from the complex life around them. The schools must learn to communicate with the community's other public and private agencies and to join in a coordinated, concerted effort.

School dollars will be in short supply for a long, long time—particularly in the city. Some of our effort must therefore go into correcting the imbalance in the economics of the city school as affected by state policies. At the same time, we must constantly seek ways to stretch those dollars that are available.

One promising route lies through what might be called cooperative packaging, by which I mean coordinating programs so that they serve double or triple functions. We must learn to look at a problem, analyze it, and put together a package that coordinates every possible resource—not just those available from the U. S. Office of Education and not just those that are specifically educational. Working relationships must be established with a range of other groups and organizations, public and private alike. This kind of intermingling of interests has advantages that go beyond economic efficiency, vital as that is. It provides new stimulation and new understanding, an opportunity to share common concerns and perhaps to arrive at some new approaches together.

An anti-dropout campaign jointly designed and administered by the schools and such groups as the Urban League, the local Community Action Agency, the PTA, and the Boys Clubs seems almost certain to reach and hold more youngsters than one conducted by the schools alone. One that uses dropouts themselves in its planning and recruitment may be even more successful, even though its planners will have some difficult meetings.

We desperately need new ideas if we are to solve the financial as well as the social and cultural problems of the cities. There is a very real danger that even if we had twice as much money available to us, these additional funds might make relatively little difference. They might simply be dissipated in doing more of the same.

When I speak of the critical need for new ideas, I am by no means suggesting that we scrap the American system of education and begin again. That system has served us well. Rather, I am thinking of the necessity of developing approaches and techniques capable of helping us deal with an array of challenges and situations that are without precedent in American society—challenges and situations that are most dramatically apparent in the cities.

Conceding that there are few genuinely new ideas, there remains the possibility of developing new uses of old ideas and of applying to city schools some of the techniques that have proved effective in other settings or endeavors. I'd like to suggest a couple of things that seem to me to fall in such a category, with no implication that any one of them or that all of them together are necessarily the panacea for a particular city. I would remind you that what may be a rousing success in San Francisco may not work at all in Detroit; that what flops miserably in Atlanta may be the answer for Rochester.

1. Consortia, such as are developing on the college level, might be developed for junior and senior high schools—perhaps even for elementary schools. All schools could have open enrollment, and students would attend several in a given day or week. The advantages might include a stronger curriculum, the elimination of duplication, and instant desegregation.

2. Pupil-teacher ratios might be established at a level of 20 to 1, at only slightly greater cost than the present arrangement, if we had each group of 20 attend class half a day instead of each

group of 35 attend class all day—and provided there are opportunities for the group not in class to study, use language labs
and computer instruction, and go on field trips chaperoned by
volunteers and teacher aides.

3. Space might be made available in ghetto schools for such
commercial establishments as grocery stores and beauty parlors,
thereby providing new services to the community, part-time job
opportunities for students, and extra revenue for the school system.

4. Students might be offered a new set of choices, so that no
student is confronted with the rigid alternatives of either being
in school full time or out of school altogether. It seems to me a
strange affair to require every boy and girl to be full-time ma-
triculating students, without regard to individual needs and interests and problems, and to offer part-time programs to youngsters only when they have encountered such social disasters as
pregnancy or jail or dropout. Perhaps we need to develop a range
of options, both in attendance requirements and in the kinds
of programs that lead to the diploma. The combinations of work
and study which can be offered to high school students are infinitely variable, and most of them remain unexplored by many
high schools.

5. We might subsidize local craftsmen—for example, potters,
silversmiths, painters, and printers—by providing rent-free space
in the schools with the proviso that they conduct a class or two in
their specialty each day.

6. We vitally need a new approach to involving the parent in
his child's life as a student and in the school itself. Too often,
to the ghetto resident the school is a hostile fortress of white authority. Too often, the parent has little faith in either the school
or the learning process. And too often, the parent does not understand his necessary role as a counselor, as a reader of stories,
or simply as a person interested in his child's school life. We need
to give parents a part in school planning, school decisions, and
school operations. For school boards, principals, and teachers,
such involvement must go far beyond a PTA tea party or the

once-a-year school open house. It means permanently established programs in which parents become a part of the formal school structure, as aides and as participants in the decision-making process.

7. New kinds of school district organization might be developed, in which some or all school district functions were decentralized. Metropolitan school boards that went all the way and established sub-districts within their system might very well find that they gained a better handle on policy; for, as you well know, the larger a district, the more likely that policy decisions are made by administrators. School boards might look to several kinds of subcontractors when considering the development of such a subsystem—educational corporations, foundations, universities, the National Education Association, the American Federation of Teachers, local community groups, and perhaps others. In the beginning of any such arrangement, some contractors would probably do well, some might do badly. In either event, this kind of decentralization could, for the first time, bring to school administration the healthy competition that, it is hardly necessary to point out, has done pretty well by the free enterprise system. And at least equally important, it could be an effective mechanism for involving parents in the conduct of the schools.

Here in the District of Columbia, the Board of Education has unanimously approved such an experiment. This year Antioch College will run two inner-city schools as community schools, under contract to the Board, and its plans call for a subsystem school board whose membership includes parents, teachers, and students. The inclusion of parents and students on a subsystem board may not be the only way to help the community and the schools become mutually responsive, but I haven't heard of a better one.

I offer these suggestions more as examples of the kind of thinking we need to do about the problems we have in our schools than as complete prescriptions for immediate success. The fact is, however, that school boards and superintendents working together face decisions which will do much to determine the shape of public education for years to come. The melancholy conclusion an impartial observer would reach is that these decisions too often reflect a tendency to do things in the schools as we have always done them even though the traditional approaches don't seem to serve the pupils with the toughest problems.

It seems to me that city school board members have the most creative and exciting policy job in the country. If you are successful in finding ways to provide education that is at the same time excellent and relevant to life in our infinitely complicated, no longer unitary cities, you will have done much to preserve the strength and vitality of American Society.

If the cities fail, so in the end will the nation, and it is the schools that will in part determine the ultimate outcome. We in the federal government are committed to doing our appropriate share in providing you with resources to do the job.

As President Johnson has so well said:

The foremost goal of this Administration has been to create a legacy of educational excellence. We shall continue to pursue that goal until our schools and universities are as great as human wisdom can make them, and the doors to our classrooms are open to every American boy and girl.

# CHAPTER 22

# CHANGING THE PECKING ORDER

P ERHAPS if we could confer PH.D's
along with citizenship and a social
security number at birth, our schools
would change from credentialling agencies to incubators of culture and centers
of intellectual ferment. Barring such a
development, we need, at the very least,
to find new ways to credential people
who missed their footing on some step
of the social, economic, and educational
escalator.

From an address before the College Entrance Examination Board, Chicago,
Illinois, October 24, 1967.

# CHANGING THE PECKING ORDER

IT IS VERY PLEASANT FOR ME TO REALIZE THAT THIS evening I have the members of the College Entrance Examination Board temporarily at my mercy. I know that this heady monopoly won't last long, but as a former vice-chairman and a long time committee member I hope you will forgive me for enjoying the opportunity to speak to you at some length, on a subject of my own choosing, without fear of interruption.

I do this, of course, by virtue of my present office. Although I am no more learned and not any wiser than I was as a member of this group, being Commissioner of Education does give me a certain leverage I didn't have before. It is this leverage—or, more precisely, such criteria for leverage—that I mean to criticize this evening.

The barnyard hierarchy which chickens establish among themselves is a natural phenomenon that we all take for granted. We call it "the pecking order." It brings the larger, the stronger, or the more confident chickens to the feeding trough before the skinny, introverted ones who most need to be fed. But in the hierarchy of social and occupational dominance, prestige and authority based on academic or titular credentials are human phenomena that I am afraid we cannot afford to take for granted. It is our somewhat artificial human pecking order that requires some examination.

It seems to me extremely important to the survival and the health of America that we find ways for the institutions which control opportunity in our society to do so with a concern for those people who have been denied opportunity by the short-comings of the society.

It is of desperate importance in a viable and open social system that we learn to cherish and nurture a variety of talents with adequate appreciation for each. Secretary of Health, Education, and Welfare John Gardner pinpointed this neatly when he wrote:

> An excellent plumber is infinitely more admirable than an incompetent philosopher. The society which scorns excellence in plumbing because plumbing is a humble activity and tolerates shoddiness in philosophy because it is an exalted activity will have neither good plumbing nor good philosophy. Neither its pipes nor its theories will hold water.

I'd like to go a step further and suggest that it is not inconceivable that our excellent plumber might also have the makings of an admirable philosopher. We have no accurate way of knowing that he would not. If we think he would not (and we probably do), it is most likely because he has no degree in philosophy. Which may be a bit like saying that Socrates wasn't a good teacher because he had no teaching credential—and suggests that we have forgotten that Spinoza earned his living as a lens grinder and that Tom Edison quit school at the age of nine.

My point is that an academic degree or a diploma is a fairly good indicator of ability, but only in a negative sense—in the sense that a person who has such a degree or diploma is probably not intellectually *in*adequate.

But taking the symbol for the substance is not the hallmark of good and careful judgment or of attention to individual differences. We should never *automatically* assume that the person with some letters after his name will perform better than the person without those letters. We should never *automatically* assume that the person who has held a job precisely like one we are trying to fill will perform better than the person who has no comparable experience.

Unfortunately, people are individuals, and institutions deal in multitudes. There is never time to inspect each person, to grade him like a cut of beef, and stamp him prime, choice, or good. Administrative necessity dictates the establishment of some criteria on which to base selection.

There is considerable evidence that public policy and institutional practice make it extremely difficult for competent but uncredentialled persons to have a fair crack at competitive situations, whether they be social, vocational, or educational.

Without question we need broad minimum standards in a whole basketful of categories. And we need efficient ways to determine whether or not our applicants meet those standards. But efficiency cannot be our only criterion. No matter what system we use to evaluate people, we need to build in provisions for unique individuals and reasonable allowance for not-so-unique individuals who have some special attribute. I don't think we are terribly good at this. At almost every level, in almost all fields, we find an automatic emphasis on credentials, a routine rigidity, whether the credential under consideration is a high school diploma, a Ph.D., or a certificate from a beauty college.

Before I cast any further stones (and I intend to do so), I'd like to make it clear that the federal government is hardly blameless in this area. This Administration, under strong directive from President Johnson, has largely eliminated job discrimination against women and against minority groups. But other categories of discrimination still exist.

Let me quote from a study of equal employment opportunities within my shop, the U. S. Office of Education:

Over-all, racial discrimination is not an important problem in the Office, certainly much less prevalent than in other institutions of society, but substantial attention could be given to . . . the credential of a college degree which is evidently more important for advancement in OE than competence itself.

Elsewhere the report is more specific:

The chance of a non-college person being promoted across the grade nine-ten barrier [this refers to Civil Service categories nine and ten] is negligible, while the possibility of a college person being promoted across the barrier in a reasonable number of years (say three) is very high. OE policy appears to say that virtually no one without a college degree is capable of handling work above Civil Service grade nine.

The most heartening element of this report is the absence of racial discrimination per se within the Office, but I'm not sure our overdependence on sheepskin and degrees is not, in its own way, an inadvertent racial discrimination.

Professor S. M. Miller of New York University made this point last year in a paper called "Credentialism and the Education System." Pointing out that education once served as a means of ascendancy for the poor, he said it is now "becoming a bar to the new poor's effort to change conditions. Today the insistence on education as a prerequisite for jobs is becoming a barrier to the occupational ascendancy of today's disprivileged.

"We have become a credential society, where one's educational level is more important than what he can do. People cannot obtain jobs that they could well fill because they lack educational qualifications. Negroes who dropped out of the educational steeplechase before getting a high school diploma cannot get jobs. Employers and the better-off do not feel that there is discrimination; rather the low-educated are 'not qualified.' "

This credentialling myopia is by no means confined to the disadvantaged. In almost every occupation, at almost every level, one finds certification requirements of one kind or another locking people out of situations in which they might well be substantial contributors. This remains true, though we know that new technology changes job functions so fast that adaptability may be more essential in a prospective employee than any specific knowledge or specific training.

Classified ad columns are full of jobs for deliverymen, parking attendants, elevator operators, and so on, who need not have experience as long as they have high school diplomas. Although a high school education may not contribute much to the skill of an elevator operator, it does simplify the task of a personnel manager who knows that his applicants are likely to be conformists, if nothing more.

The official directory of the City of New York has 47 pages of

very small type that list licenses, permits, or certification requirements for such diverse occupations as midwifery, ophthalmic dis-
pensary traineeships, undertakers, oil-burner operators, and fu-
neral directors' apprentices.

A recent letter to members of a private university club in
New York City announced the appointment of a man whom I
shall fictitiously call Charles Chan as general manager. It identified him as Charles Chan, CCM. What is CCM? Certified Club
Manager.

I don't mean to suggest that I am against letters after people's
names, nor am I against any sort of effort to insure competence or
adequate skills on the part of midwives or undertakers. What
does concern me is that the route into an increasing number of
occupations is a specific educational route and, for some professions, that route begins close to infancy and makes no provision
for detours.

Author John Keats has written of the ferocious competition
for entrance to private nursery schools. In New York City, such
preschools report over 150 applications for every vacancy. This
kind of competition stems from parental concern for their children's entrance into elementary and preparatory school (which is
easier for a graduate of a "good" nursery school), and aims ultimately, of course, at entrance into a "good" college. Anxious parents have been known to hire tutors to coach three-year-olds on
the Stanford Binet test, and to change their religious affiliation to
secure placement in desirable church-sponsored schools.

Again, I'm not against private nursery schools nor against parents who want the best education for their children. My concern
is that this credential-laden rat race doesn't permit society to establish meaningful criteria and standards that apply to the population as a whole. Nor does it allow adequately for exceptions. A
society that prides itself on equality of opportunity must somehow learn to accommodate those children who are least likely to
collect adequate credentials but who may have the unrealized
potential to succeed in demanding tasks.

There are many bright children in inner-city schools. I think there is a reasonable doubt that they get a fair shake. It may well be, as Marshall McLuhan has said, that it is the bright kids who drop out because school "is not where the action is." Certainly bright people drop out of college and graduate schools. But typically our schools and colleges have acted as selection agents on an economic basis (and therefore on a racial basis) rather than as purveyors of equal opportunity.

In the last few years we have established a new doctrine for elementary and secondary education; its premise is that equal educational opportunity does not result from treating all pupils equally. The underlying basis for the Elementary and Secondary Education Act of 1965 is the conviction that our schools must do more for those pupils who come to school with less—and this includes, but is not limited to, spending more per pupil for their education.

Now it is time to ask what the colleges have done (and what they propose to do) in order to reflect this new philosophy in higher education; how they plan to give students the educational opportunities that will help them progress, and when they will forego their role as sorting out institutions serving the "haves" and ignoring the "have-nots."

We need to remember that the high school student who sticks it out because he knows he can earn almost twice as much as his dropout friend (even if his friend is brighter) isn't *always* more valuable to society than the dropout. The student who stays in college knowing that he will probably earn $150,000 more than his friend who drops out is not *necessarily* an inquiring intellect. The graduate student writing his thesis on the "Subliminal Use of Visual Symbols in 14th and 15th Century Prose and Poetry" may not be on an educational quest of much significance even though it will gain him a credential. He may be, as suggested by Kingsley Amis, engaging in the teutonic academic tradition of "casting pseudo-light on non-problems."

The promising law student, who elects a law school that confers a doctor of jurisprudence instead of electing Harvard which confers a bachelor of laws, is probably a realist. He knows that the J.D. can make him an instant assistant professor if he chooses to teach after graduation. With an LL.B., even from Harvard, he will probably only be offered an instructorship, although the course work and skills required for the LL.B. may be more demanding.

Until we learn how to tell when people are competent, we will continue to have a great many people going to school for the wrong reasons and a great many more who are *not* going to school for the wrong reasons. As managers and as admissions officers we are going to lose a lot of "mute, inglorious Miltons" unless we find some better ways to measure potential ability and unless we can serve larger numbers of people with an education which helps the individual reach the credential rather than failing him because he cannot reach it in the same fashion as others.

I don't know what the answer is. Perhaps if we could confer Ph.D.'s along with citizenship and a social security number at birth, our schools would change from credentialling agencies to incubators of culture and centers of intellectual ferment. Barring such a development, we need, at the very least, to find new ways to credential people who missed their footing on some step of the social, economic, and educational escalator.

There is a paradox here: we've committed ourselves to the credentialling system, and now we need to find ways to beat it. The institutions which are involved in it must now learn to act on behalf of the people who are affected by it. Some institutions are already beginning to take an interest in high-risk students, and the federal government is helping support their efforts through Upward Bound, Talent Search, and a number of other compensatory programs.

But institutional efforts must go beyond taking these less credentialled youngsters into their hallowed halls. The institutions will have to offer them special support services after they get there; we can't just get rid of them if they start to fail. If their intellectual foundations are weak, then we will have to do a rebuilding job. This is going to demand some major adjustments on the part of institutions—not a lowering of standards but the introduction of flexibility. If a student comes from a deprived background, the college has to read that into his record and learn to identify his talent and ability even though his test scores do not show it in conventional ways.

This also means that we have to read the disadvantaged background factor into college entrance examination scores before making decisions on admission. If we consider tests as diagnostic devices, they can be used to include, rather than exclude. Thus a youngster who is far behind in mathematics may be admitted, but required to take a special compensatory mathematics course. Perhaps colleges should add a whole year of precollege compensatory work to the regular curriculum offerings. We're all living longer nowadays. There is no reason that some of us can't take five years to get through college. If the added time will bring success, it's more than worth it.

Our country has a tremendous investment in this sort of rebuilding. We simply can't let a whole generation go by because we've just learned the lessons of Head Start and are waiting for last year's preschoolers to reach college age. We must get some of these people into colleges now so that we can graduate more Mexican-Americans and more Negroes *now*. Otherwise we are going to end up with a rigidly stratified society because the whole credentialling system serves the middle class and rejects the less fortunate.

All our carefully developed forms of exclusion might make economic (if not moral) sense if society was oversupplied with skilled manpower. At a time when we face desperate shortages in almost all professions and skilled trades, it is wasteful and dangerous. Let's take teaching as an example. Accumulated data from elementary and secondary school districts across the nation show a shortage of over 200,000 certified teachers. What does that mean? What does it take to be a certified teacher? If we move from locality to locality, from coast to coast, we find a conflicting array of certification requirements. Do they make sense? Often they do. But let's examine an individual instance.

A woman in her late twenties, a graduate of Smith College,

had taught English successfully in a French school in Paris for
two years, had been an editorial assistant on *Réalités* for one year
and had taught French in a private preparatory school in Pennsylvania for two years. She moved to another state and applied
for a job teaching French in a suburban, public elementary
school. I don't need to tell you what happened. No job, because
of lack of credentials. I probably don't need to tell you, either,
that a majority of states do not require language teachers to be
able to speak the language they are to teach; an unfortunately
large number of language teachers cannot do so.

I am sure there is an abundance of qualified but uncredentialled (note that I resist saying the reverse—credentialled but
unqualified) talent available to the elementary and secondary
school classrooms of this nation. But the benefits of this talent
will continue to elude us as long as we are locked into a rigid
credentialling system that permits us, out of fear, laziness, or
irresponsibility, to abandon the exercise of judgment when we
make decisions about people.

I might add that there are signs of a breakthrough on the
credential problem. Although I know some congressmen who
would not consider it a virtue, both President Kennedy and President Johnson have set an example by appointing Commissioners
of Education who lacked an advanced degree. On the other side
of the coin is the fact that neither of these Commissioners can
meet the new credentials of the American Association of School
Administrators.

Those who are already established in a profession or occupation are usually responsible for maintaining its standards. When
a credentialling review committee is established, somehow its
members always come up with tougher entrance requirements.
Rarely does anyone ever suggest making it easier to get in and
point out the possibility of getting some good people that way.

It is human nature to want to keep our club hard to get into;
logic always loses when the ego is threatened. Even public relations, the last refuge for eclectic self-educated talent (after metropolitan newspapers began requiring journalism degrees for

copyboys), recently instituted tough credentialling procedures—so tough that only 17 percent of the present members of the national society were able to pass the examination. Nonetheless, new applicants will have to do so or the national society won't accept them.

These are not frivolous matters. When we determine the educational and vocational limits of individual lives by such practices, procedures, and symbols, we not only do injustice to the individual but we inflict a potential talent loss of inestimable consequence to the nation. What can we do about it? We certainly cannot do away with credentials—they are as much a part of the contemporary scene as taxes and television (and I have mixed feelings about all three).

But we can minimize their impact of a negative kind by having the wisdom to use them wisely and flexibly. We can, as I said earlier, develop some new ways to acquire them. Several federal programs focus on this problem. They are aimed at developing new careers for the poor, jobs that provide semiprofessional status in the fields of medicine and education. We *can* do this; we can break down the professional role so that subprofessional jobs open up. More importantly we can relate the subprofessional role to the professional so that a person can shift from one to the other with greater ease. There are plenty of teacher aides and nurses' aides who would make good teachers or good nurses if we could provide special training programs for them and persuade the professional establishment to accept their ability to perform professional tasks despite the absence of some of the traditionally required credentials.

We can give more credit for experience, both in hiring people and in selecting them for educational institutions. An example: When the State University of New York opens its experimental college next year, it plans to give undergraduate credit for Peace Corps experience.

Colleges and universities might relax entrance requirements for master's degree candidates. Gifted college dropouts with ten or fifteen years subsequent experience who wish to enter a master's degree program should, perhaps, be able to get a waiver of their undergraduate degree.

We must remember that some people will learn whether or not they have the advantage of college experience; that some other people, if they have staying power, can end up with degrees that really don't mean much.

We can continue to search for better ways to evaluate people, more sophisticated ways to measure ability, skill, and potential. And, finally, we can build escape clauses into all our certifying, credentialling, and admissions procedures to allow individual consideration of people with special situations, unique talents, or measurable handicaps.

None of this is enough to change the pecking order radically, but if we are conscientious in our effort to look at people, not paper, and offer honest second chances educationally and professionally, we may be able to help a few skinny chickens get a little closer to the feeding trough.

# CHAPTER 23

# NATIONAL IDEALS AND EDUCATIONAL POLICY

T HE NOTION of "equality" has never
been static and fixed for us. Time
and circumstance have forced us to revise past definitions. In this political
sense, therefore, the United States is as
much a developing nation as the newest
member of the United Nations.

From an address before the National Conference on Race and Education, sponsored by the U. S. Commission on Civil Rights, Washington, D. C., November 17, 1967.

# NATIONAL IDEALS AND EDUCATIONAL POLICY

THE OLD TESTAMENT TELLS US THAT THE SINS OF fathers are visited on their sons. Presuming for the moment that this lugubrious sentiment is valid, it seems to me it ought to be amended to include virtues as well; the United States has been suffering for almost two centuries now from the idealism of the founding fathers.

The particular ideals I have in mind are stated, among other places, in the second sentence of the Declaration of Independence: "We hold these truths to be self-evident, that all men are created equal. . . ."

Having enunciated those familiar words, I realize that I run the risk of exciting your irritation. You may suspect that they are the prelude to a superficially patriotic sermon, a hearty injunction for all of us to stop this silly bickering and remember that we are all brothers.

These words are a prelude to something, of course, but not— I hope—to a set of simplistic pieties. The problems of achieving equal opportunity in education or in any other aspect of our national life are much too complex to be resolved by mere good feeling. I quote these words as much out of desperation as conviction. Desperation because, wondering whether there is anything new to say about race and education, I thought I'd explore something old. And conviction because it seems to me that perhaps our national ideals—apart from furnishing us with some memorable prose—have a more definite function and force than is commonly supposed.

One of the consequences of discovering, as most of us do, that ideals have often been ignored or exploited in the past is to make one wonder whether they have any value at all. Are they merely a decorative wallpaper to spruce up a society's house, or do they keep out some heat and cold as well? Are they simply graceful formulations handy for cloaking a nation's pragmatic self-interest in the garments of justice and virtue—or do they contain within them, perhaps to a degree we cannot measure, some philosophical and psychological energies that help explain a nation's present strength?

Such speculations are inevitable, and every responsible citizen must engage in them. One possibility is to conclude that ideals are indeed little more than baubles—tinseled stars for the naive to aim their hearts at while the canny movers and shakers of the real world get the work done. Another possibility is to conclude that, while ideals are rarely realized in their fullness, the exercise of attempting to achieve them renews a society's strength, and that a nation which turns its back on high aspirations does so at peril of increasing weakness.

This matter of equality has been giving us trouble ever since the Declaration of Independence was published. Every succeeding generation has tried to figure out, in the context of its own times, what our forefathers meant by stating that "All men are created equal." Since common observation tells us the reverse every day, we have concluded that only in a special sense can all men be considered equals. Broadly stated, it means that as Americans they are entitled to equality under the law in preserving life and liberty, and in seeking happiness.

Yet even that restricted formulation has given us trouble. At one time, a person's right to all the privileges of American citizenship hinged on ownership of property, and, at another time, on sex: it took us more than a century to decide that women could vote.

So it is clear that defining equality in the United States has been an evolutionary process, one by which we have erased one special characteristic after another from the list of criteria for full citizenship. The notion of "equality" has never been static and fixed for us. Time and circumstance have forced us to revise past definitions. In this political sense, therefore, the United States is as much a developing nation as the newest member of the United Nations.

Without question, the single characteristic that has given us the most trouble throughout this enterprise is that of race. The Thirteenth, Fourteenth, and Fifteenth Amendments started the job, but we have not finished it yet. We are here to consider how much remains to be done, and how to go about it, particularly in the schools. This conference proceeds from two facts: first, equality before the law—the right to life, liberty, and the pursuit of happiness—is meaningless without an equal right to an excellent education; second, for an American citizen, segregated education cannot be excellent.

Thirteen years ago, the Supreme Court recognized the intrinsic relationship between equality of education and equality of citizenship when it decided that segregated education is of its nature unequal and decreed that desegregation of schools should proceed with "all deliberate speed." As has often been remarked, the implementation of this decision has been characterized more by deliberation than by speed. And yet, despite the snail's pace of school desegregation, the snail has slowly picked up speed as parents, civil rights groups, and the courts have begun enforcing the 1954 decision. Since 1964 the Civil Rights Act has provided a basis for further efforts. Three years ago, in the Old South and in the border states, less than 2 percent of the 3½ million Negro youngsters had any white classmates at all. Since then we have multiplied that figure by more than eight times, to more than 16 percent.

More important for the future of desegregation, the federal judiciary this year backed the position taken by the Departments of Justice and Health, Education, and Welfare that measurable progress is the sole test of a desegregation plan. This ruling means that school districts will no longer be able to use freedom-of-choice desegregation plans as a basis for compliance with the

Civil Rights Act unless such plans actually work to eliminate the dual school system.

In sum, that system is on the way out. It will take more time before it disappears completely, and before its effects on white and non-white individuals educated under it cease to influence each other's lives. Yet there is hardly a responsible official in the country who still maintains that public policy and support should maintain separate school systems for different races. This is a genuine gain.

Today, however, we are increasingly concerned with school segregation in the cities, where our great concentrations of minorities live. And we are concerned in the cities with a form of segregation which grows not from dual schools but from patterns of living. The issues we confront in this type of segregation consume our energies, cast a shadow on our ideals, and confront us with a major argument about public policy.

On the one side of this argument are those who say that desegregation simply cannot be brought about in the near future. They point to Washington, D. C., with a Negro school population of over 90 percent, to New York City and Chicago, with their 50 percent non-white school populations, and say that there just are not enough white youngsters to go around to produce desegregation. Therefore, they say, let's forget the impossible; let's concentrate enough money and services and experienced teachers in the ghetto schools to make them the best in the city, even if they *are* segregated. In effect, this viewpoint presents the case for schools which are separate, but *unequal*—unequal in the sense that they do more for minority group children than they do for the fortunate white majority.

On the other side are those who say that big-city segregation is per se so bad—so destructive of the children caught up in it—that compensatory education cannot begin to alleviate its evils. Segregation, they say, denies a child the privilege of thinking of himself as a first-class citizen; no matter how excellent an education such a school offers him in an academic sense, it denies him that sense of equality with other children, that sense of personal dignity and self-confidence which is so important to achievement in school and beyond. Therefore, goes this side of the argument, let's bring every kind of legal, financial, and political pressure to bear on the single goal of integration, because that is the only solution to inequality of educational opportunity. According to this view, the only way Negroes will ever get good schools is to join the children whose white parents control the quality of the schools.

The proponents of both viewpoints can marshal platoons of statistics to support their contentions. I am not competent to evaluate this evidence or, for that reason, to argue from it. Neither, I might add, are many of the people who are quoting these figures most vociferously. But I am convinced—on the basis of common sense and on the basis of what our country professes to stand for—that we make a mistake to espouse either of these courses to the exclusion of the other.

It is obvious, as the advocates of compensatory education point out, that we cannot achieve full desegregation tomorrow. In some cities, where non-white school populations approach or exceed 50 percent, it is unlikely that we will have integrated schools for another generation. Yet no matter how unrealistic desegregation may seem in such cities, I must question whether compensatory education of the quality we seek is much easier to achieve.

Consider for a moment what we are talking about when we recommend compensatory education as the only answer. If it is to be genuine compensatory education—education that makes up for the failings of the home and for an entire heritage of failure and self-doubt—we are probably talking about massive per-pupil expenditures, about providing a great variety of special services ranging from health and psychological care to remedial education efforts. We are talking about remaking the relationship between the school and the home, and between the school and employment opportunity. We are talking about identifying and appointing that essential person who is in such short supply—the inspiring elementary school principal. We are talking about arrangements for retraining most teachers and for putting a city's best and most experienced instructors in its ghetto schools which now get more than their share of uncertified, inexperienced, temporary teachers. We are talking about new curricular materials, some untried and some yet to be developed, as well as about revised methods of instruction. Particularly in the large cities of the East, we are talking about replacing school plants which, on the average, are nearly a quarter century older than schools outside the city. And we are considering doing all these things for children whose families are on the move, children in schools where the enrollment often changes radically from year to year.

The school systems on which we would impose these tasks are underfinanced, beset by self-appointed critics with every conceivable viewpoint, and ill-supported by the states in which they exist. Certainly they have faults, but the major responsibility for those faults lies not on the doorstep of harrassed school officials; rather, it rests with every one of us who has paid lip service to the importance of public education while allowing it to deteriorate.

With resources from the federal government, we have two years of initial effort behind us on this task of remaking education in the central city. We cannot at this point scientifically measure what we have achieved, but we know that there are hopeful signs. When President Johnson and the 89th Congress created a new alliance between the federal government and the public schools, they took on no easy job for either party. They committed themselves to a long, difficult, expensive task of experimentation, service, and change—a task perhaps as difficult as desegregation.

In the practical sense, then, I do not think we have two alternatives. We must pursue both compensatory education and desegregated schools at the same time. And this is not, I hasten to point out, a prescription for fence-straddling or an invitation to inaction. A number of local school boards, given the option of using federal funds to improve their schools, have chosen to couple compensatory programs with devices for increasing integration at the same time.

• In Pittsburgh, the school administration is building five
Great High Schools, each designed to serve a student population
of about 5,000 from every social, economic, ethnic, and national
group in the city. At the same time that these schools eliminate
segregated student societies, they will also produce higher quality
education through bringing new resources to the service of all
students.

• In White Plains, New York, the school board decided in
1964 to attack *de facto* segregation. Every school, the board decided, would have no less than a 10 percent Negro enrollment
and no more than 30 percent. In a recent study, the school system
concluded that the program had benefited both white and Negro
students academically and that it has not led to any exodus of
white students from the public schools.

• In Evanston, Illinois, the school system has committed itself to a desegregation plan that will give every elementary school
a Negro enrollment of between 15 and 25 percent. One feature of
the plan, the conversion of a formerly all-Negro school to an integrated laboratory school operated in conjunction with North-
western University, has been so popular that there is a waiting
list of white parents anxious to send their children there.

• In Berkeley, California, the school system has launched a
program that combines busing with special instruction provided
by parents, university graduate students, community volunteers,
and an increased staff to blend compensatory education and desegregation. Now under consideration by the school board is a
plan that would desegregate all the city's schools next fall by
classroom exchanges involving 4,300 of the district's 9,000 elementary school children.

Each of these efforts has been partially financed by federal
funds. Not one of them, however, was dictated by federal policy
or requirement. They are examples of community responsibility
exercised on behalf of minority group Americans by enlightened
local leadership. Most school boards today at least have the problem of segregation on their agenda. These school boards I have

mentioned, as well as numerous others, are doing something about it. Ten years ago the segregation problem was not on the agenda at all except in a very few places.

We are faced with a variety of forms of segregation in American cities, each with peculiar local circumstances. A plan that works in White Plains, with 17 percent Negro student population, would be absurd in Washington, D. C., with over 90 percent. Plans for either of those cities would make little sense in Denver, where public education officials must accommodate a significant minority of Spanish-speaking children, as well as Negro and white children. Large cities have more aggravated and less manageable problems than medium-sized cities.

Perhaps in some cities, compensatory efforts will have earlier effect than those aimed at desegregation. In our basic policy commitments, however, we have no choice except to plan for and strive for desegregated schools. Compensatory education, whatever its immediate values, is only a partial measure. Although it encourages integration of the schools in the long run by improving services for all children, it offers no answer for the young people who must wait in segregated schools for the millennium to arrive. We cannot allow the fact that the solution may be years ahead to erase the problem of segregation from our priority lists now.

What are the long-term prospects for desegregated schools?

I do not think we will ever have genuinely integrated education until we have a genuinely desegregated society. And such a society—one in which every man is free to succeed or fail on his merits, to qualify for a job on the basis of his ability alone, to live where he chooses as long as he can pay the rent or make the mortgage payment—seems a long way off. We have made progress in every one of these areas during the 1960's, but we have far to go. The question that confronts us is whether we can move fast enough in the years immediately ahead to keep the hopes our small progress has generated from turning into bitter frustration and hate.

It is a curious thing that a little progress often brings a disproportionate amount of frustration, anger, and violence. Every white person knows other whites who, reacting to the riots in our cities and to the continual demands of our deprived minorities, ask, "What more do *they* want?" And every black person, I suppose, knows at least one Negro who proclaims his willingness to blow the country up tomorrow if Whitey does not come across today.

Such white reactions, in the case of persons who felt at least an initial sympathy with the civil rights movement, stem partially from a defective sense of our nation's history. Resenting a riot, of course, does not require any historical sense; a riot is just plain wrong. But whites who ask, "Why don't they *work* their way up the way we did?" might be chagrined to discover that American Negroes *are* "working their way up" in a fashion not dissimilar to that previously engaged in by a number of white minorities— through a combination of strenuous toil, political pressure, and outbreaks of violence.

We must realize, it seems to me, that American Negroes were denied any legitimate outlet for their special interests during the first 200 years of their residence here, and that for the next century, their rights as citizens were more theoretical than real. Now, with the support of the administration, the last two Congresses and the federal courts, American Negroes have fought for and gained their first real vision of the possibilities of justice. For 300 years they have had no hope; now they have not only hope but also some tangible fruits to prove the value of hope. It is not in the least surprising that they should resent even 24 hours more of delay.

But the legitimate uses of power and the understandable frustrations of American Negroes do not justify the cries of those on the violent fringe who advocate extorting justice through destruction. It is as important for such extremists to realize that they are delaying the day of complete equality as it is for whites to realize that these extremists consist only of the clamorous few.

Both Negro extremism and extreme white reaction to it complicate the major social dilemma of our lives. When we view the various obstacles standing between us and a genuinely open society, I suspect many of us at times are tempted to lose our nerve and our determination to follow through on the course we began plotting in 1954. Members of the majority may question whether achieving *any* ideal is worth the turmoil that this particular ideal has already cost us. Members of minority groups, knowing that they are outnumbered, may worry whether, at some point, the majority will say, "Enough. We are not yet ready for integration. The clock will have to stand still for another generation."

It is at this point that I would return to my earlier remarks about the force and function of an ideal. The ideal of equality has given Americans trouble ever since our nation was founded—not just as regards Negro Americans but with other minorities as well. It has pushed us into one bitter controversy after another, sometimes setting American against American and generating vast amounts of hostility. It has picked fights for us, fights that many men in every time would have preferred to avoid.

But we have won each of those fights. Each victory has renewed our national energies, renewed our national conviction that we *can* lick our problems one by one. We know that the experience of failure has a profound effect on an individual: if repeated again and again, it makes him doubt his own abilities. The experience of repeated success has an analogous effect: it makes a man capable of daring greater things than he would normally attempt.

I suspect that experience develops a similar sense of invincibility or of inability in nations. We, the people of the United States, by having the courage to confront at various times in our history the most agonizing problems of social policy and domestic practice, have built up a winning streak that has enabled us to face fear at home and abroad with quiet confidence in our own ability to win once again.

At this time in our history, we face another crisis of national courage. We face a fight which, in the belief of many Americans, it would be nice to avoid. Do we really have to go through this again when, for most of us, life is reasonably comfortable? Do we really have to sustain these battles over busing and school redistricting and teacher assignment? Do we have to scrap all the time about open housing ordinances and equal employment opportunity; do we have to penalize ourselves for more taxes? Isn't there any way to avoid such a grievous, expensive, tiring, and passionate exercise as desegregating America?

There is not. The legacy of our national ideals leaves us no choice of goals. The argument over the educational merits of desegregation is, in a sense, irrelevant. It is fortunate that studies of the effects of desegregated education show us that certain learning gains emerge from it. But even if the studies disclosed no such gains, we would *still* be morally committed to desegregation.

It seems to me that in designing school policy which responds to that commitment—that constructively serves youngsters from both the minority and the majority groups—we have three fundamental propositions to keep in mind.

1. Local boards of education must accept their responsibility for using all the resources at their command—federal and state as well as local—to improve education and reduce segregation at the same time. These local boards confront countless decisions each year on such questions as location of schools, the design of facilities, teacher assignment policies, and school organization patterns. These issues are not separate unto themselves, or at least need not be. The possible alternatives can also bear on educational improvement and school desegregation. I would hope that school boards would keep these two goals constantly in mind in all their decisions, and address them simultaneously and with equal vigor.

2. State departments of education must begin to accept more responsibility for school desegregation as they develop a greater capacity for improving quality. Some departments—in those states which maintained dual school systems—have begun to do so, after being prodded by the federal government. Some others, including Michigan, California, Massachusetts, New York, and Connecticut, have exercised leadership in school desegregation of their own free will. Nevertheless, such state departments are a distinct minority.

3. The federal government must continue vigorously to carry out the provisions of Titles IV and VI of the Civil Rights Act. I can guarantee that this will happen under the new administrative arrangements set up in the Department of Health, Education, and Welfare for Title VI responsibility. Plans are under way for nationwide policy guides to Title VI so that school districts in the North and in the South have a clearer picture of their obligations. The federal government must also encourage the constructive use of the programs it makes available to states and localities as leverage which can at the same time improve education and promote the desegregation of schools. The federal government literally cannot and certainly should not demand reductions of segregation beyond those required by law. At the same time, since equality of educational opportunity is closely connected to the removal of segregation, the federal government must not stand in the way of decisions by local school districts and by individual states to pursue desegregation as an essential element in improving their schools.

To assist states and local agencies in this effort, I can announce today that we are strengthening operations of Title IV of the Civil Rights Act. We have created a new Division of Equal Educational Opportunities in the Bureau of Elementary and Secondary Education. We are providing this new division with 70 new staff persons to provide greatly increased technical assistance to local agencies requesting their service. More than half of the enlarged staff will be assigned to regional Office of Education offices to be available to work directly in the field.

Only if the agencies in this country responsible for the conduct of our schools move simultaneously toward quality education and equal educational opportunity will they give practical meaning to the proposition with which we started this discussion, the splendid American proposition "that all men are created equal." Maintaining the ideals that accompanied this nation's birth demands a dedication to law and principle that we are once again called upon to display.

**DATE DUE**

| | | | |
|---|---|---|---|
| | | | |
| | | | |
| | | | |
| | | | |
| | | | |
| | | | |
| | | | |
| | | | |
| | | | |
| | | | |
| | | | |
| | | | |